important!
p155

His Gentle Voice

BY JUDITH COUCHMAN

His Gentle Voice

A Garden's Promise

The Woman Behind the Mirror

Shaping a Woman's Soul

Designing a Woman's Life Bible Study

Designing a Woman's Life

Lord, Please Help Me to Change

Lord, Have You Forgotten Me?

Why Is Her Life Better Than Mine?

If I'm So Good, Why Don't I Act That Way?

Getting a Grip on Guilt

COMPILATIONS BY JUDITH COUCHMAN

The Promise of Power (Jamie Buckingham)

One Holy Passion (Female Authors)

Breakfast for the Soul (Various Authors)

Only Trust Him (Dwight L. Moody)

For Me to Live Is Christ (Charles Spurgeon)

Growing Deeper with God (Oswald Chambers)

Dare to Believe (Smith Wigglesworth)

Anywhere He Leads Me (Corrie ten Boom)

Loving God with All Your Heart (Andrew Murray)

A Very Present Help (Amy Carmichael)

His Gentle Voice

Listening for God
in Everyday Moments

JUDITH COUCHMAN

MULTNOMAH PUBLISHERS
Sisters, Oregon

HIS GENTLE VOICE
published by Multnomah Publishers, Inc.

and in association with the literary agency of Alive Communications,
1465 Kelly Johnson Blvd., Suite 320, Colorado Springs, CO 80920

© 1998 Judith C. Couchman
Cover photograph © 1998 by Photonica
International Standard Book Number: 1-57673-076-X
Printed in the United States of America
Unless otherwise noted, Scripture quotations are from
The Holy Bible, New International Version © 1973, 1984 by International Bible Society,
used by permission of Zondervan Publishing House.
Also quoted: *New American Standard Bible* © 1960, 1977 by the Lockman Foundation.
The Holy Bible, New Century Version © 1991 by Word Publishing.
The Holy Bible, New King James Version © 1984 by Thomas Nelson, Inc.
The Holy Bible, King James Version.
The Living Bible © 1971. Used by permission of Tyndale House Publishers, Inc.
All rights reserved.
The Amplified Bible © 1965 by Zondervan Publishing House. All Rights Reserved

Multnomah is a trademark of Multnomah Publishers and is registered in the U.S. Trademark and Patent office. the colophon is a trademark of Multnomah Publishers, Inc.

No part of this publication may be reproduced, stored in a retrieval system, or
transmitted, in any form or by any means—electronic, mechanical,
photocopying, recording, or otherwise—without prior written permission.
For information:
MULTNOMAH PUBLISHERS, INC.
POST OFFICE BOX 1720
SISTERS, OREGON 97759

Library of Congress Cataloging-in-Publication Data:
Couchman, Judith, 1953–
    His Gentle Voice: listening for God in everyday moments/by Judith Couchman.
    p.cm.   ISBN 1-57673-076-X (alk. paper)   1. Spiritual life—Christianity.
    2. Listening—Religious aspects—Christianity.   I. Title.
        BV4501.2.C683   1998   98-13887   248.4—dc21   CIP

98 99 00 01 02 03 04 — 10 9 8 7 6 5 4 3 2 1

For Nancy Lemons,
my forever friend

❧

If we wish to know Him, we may hear His gentle voice saying, "Come and see."

CHARLES SPURGEON

Contents

Acknowledgments

When an author collaborates on five books with the same editor, either the relationship is exceptional or somebody is codependent. Fortunately for me, my author-editor bond with Carol Bartley is a gift to be treasured, growing richer through the years and welling up as a source of constant learning.

Carol is the detail person I am not, and though I jokingly called her the "Word Police," I know that when she reviews my manuscript, it is in loving and capable hands. Her insights improve a book's readability and sensibility, and without her pragmatism I'd probably descend into metaphors so obscure no reader would follow me there. Carol possesses the remarkable ability to critique my work, even tell me unpleasant news, in a manner so gracious I think I've just been complimented. She has a case of perennial politeness from which I hope she never recovers. It is greatly needed in the publishing industry and the world. Most of all, Carol has turned into a warm and trusted friend. For all she does for me, for all that she is, I deeply thank her.

I also thank my prayer team members who, along with my mother, Opal Couchman, her friend Mae Lammers, and my sister, Shirley Honeywell, have supported me through twenty-two books. They are Charette Barta, Win Couchman, Madalene Harris, Karen Hilt, and Nancy Lemons. All are serious intercessors. All are lifelong friends.

There are many others who through the years have supported me in the adventures of book writing, but at this juncture I especially thank Joan Badzik, Betty Bradley, Mary Brosa, Deena Davis, Janel Ferguson, Liz Heaney, Melissa Honeywell, Andy Landis, Beth Lueders, Marian McFadden, Traci Mullins, Anne Scott, Naomi Trujillo Smith, Connie Swanson, Darleen Paglialonga, Rebecca Price, and Kathe Wunnenberg who have significantly "been there" for me during the birthing of this book. Thank you for echoing God's voice and extending His love.

Introduction

For over thirty years Margaret has been one of my mother's dearest friends. Margaret attended the tiny church of my youth, and she frequently talked about how much she loved God. She often said, "Isn't the Lord good?" as more of a statement than a question and spent hours reading her well-worn Bible. Margaret also seemed to possess a special connection to God, receiving poignant answers to her prayers and hearing specific guidance from Him. She talked with Jesus as if He were standing next to her in the flesh and His voice sounded gentle and kind.

As a young teenager I bumped into conflicting feelings about Margaret's communication with God. I wanted to run away from her. I wanted to be just like her. Although this is a common response to godliness, back then I only knew that Margaret had something I wasn't sure I could get. To me, she lived "up there" in the mountaintop experiences of apostles and prophets. I wandered the foothills. At the same time, Margaret was pragmatic and approachable. A widow, she struggled with the emotions and practicalities of finances, the trials of raising a teenage daughter, her own shortcomings, and encroaching loneliness. Yet she brimmed with hugs and good words for "folks," and people easily loved her.

How can she be so close to God yet so down to earth? I asked myself, as if the two were mutually exclusive.

Margaret's most profound influence on me—and all those who knew her—occurred several years after her husband's death when her son, daughter-in-law, and two grandchildren were killed in a head-on car collision. In unutterable pain she smiled through the tears and said, "We can trust the Lord." I could only guess that her straight talk with God was comforting and holding her up. How else could she have put one foot in front of the other?

I live many miles away now, but I'm always pleased when Mom says she's spent a day with Margaret. The two women are affected by some distance and the slowing down of age, so they meet only occasionally, but they are still soul mates. I know their days together fill with talk about children and grandchildren, projects and prayer requests, and most of all Jesus, who Margaret still believes is incredibly good. Mom returns from these visits happy and encouraged, as she should be. Visiting Margaret also means spending time with God.

❧

How have we acquired the idea that God reserves His communication for "perfect" and "super spiritual" Christians and not everyday, flawed people like ourselves? Perhaps we've been mistaught about God's ways with humanity. Maybe the notion is part of passed-along Christian folklore. Or perhaps it reveals our personal insecurities and misconceptions of God's character. However the idea originated, it is not biblical.

Undoubtedly God can and does communicate through extra-

ordinary means and mountaintop experiences, through times of solitude and pulling away from the world. But God is everywhere and can
speak anywhere. He calls out appointed prophets and contemplatives,
but most often He wants His people to become Margarets, carrying
His guidance and affirmation into the encounters and commitments of
real-world lives.

Accordingly, God speaks to us in the midst of our days, in the
places where we live and work and pray, be they quiet or chaotic. Still,
we need to learn to listen, not with fear or formulas but with open,
tender, expectant hearts. The Quaker statesman William Penn wrote,
"Men may tire themselves in a labyrinth of search, and talk of God; but
if we would know Him indeed, it must be from the impressions we
receive of Him; and the softer our hearts are, the deeper and livelier
those will be upon us."[1]

My hope is that these pages will encourage you toward discovering this truth—so in the everyday moments you'll hear His gentle
voice.

Judith Couchman

Chapter One

The Hearing Heart

❧

When we believe that God lovingly seeks our best
and that He is vastly more sensitive to us
than we are to ourselves, we will seek to hear Him.
When we doubt God's intentions, His intimate caring,
or His ability to speak directly and work powerfully in our lives,
we may go through the motions...
but [we] won't be listening expectantly for God.

MARTHA THATCHER

Hannah was a desperate woman.

Year after year when she packed for the annual trip to Shiloh with her husband, Elkanah, her heart filled with dread. There they would present sacrifices and offerings to the Lord in His house. There they would celebrate Jehovah's goodness to them. There, once again, Hannah would feel humiliated.

"But why?" asked Elkanah, cupping Hannah's face in his weathered hands and kissing the lips he adored. "Why are you so sad? Why can't you enjoy our trip to the holy temple?"

Hannah tried to explain, for she deeply loved her husband, but the words jumbled, and her eyes puddled with tears. Moving his hands to Hannah's back and pulling her to his chest, Elkanah implored, "Why, my dear wife?"

With her head tucked under his chin, she sobbed, "I speak to the Lord, and He does not talk back to me. Nor does He answer my pleas for a child."

Elkanah sighed and kissed the top of Hannah's head. "Don't I mean more to you than ten sons?" he asked quietly.

"You are everything a husband can mean to a wife," she answered. "But I cannot extinguish my desire to conceive. It burns within me."

Hannah was not ungrateful for Elkanah's attention or his husbandly protection and provision. Many women in her hill community endured their marriages; their spouses treated them as mere chattel, as objects to own rather than lovers to cherish. But not Elkanah. He delighted in Hannah and favored her. Each year when he sacrificed to the Lord, Elkanah gave portions of the meat to his other wife, Peninnah, and to all her sons and daughters. But to Hannah he gave a double portion as a symbol of his enduring love, even with Peninnah's jealous eyes watching him. Even though Hannah bore him no children.

Yet as much as he tried, Elkanah couldn't understand the depth of Hannah's pain. The maternal instinct, deep as the soul itself. The shame when neighbors insinuated her barrenness was God's curse for some secret sin. The taunting from the "other woman" in Elkanah's life who plentifully bore him heirs and sneered at infertility. The desire to complete her marriage—to express her love with the greatest gift she could give, the birth of a son.

Perhaps Elkanah didn't want to feel the pain, for fear it would tear him asunder. Perhaps he was busy in the fields and oblivious to Hannah's daily troubles, as husbands sometimes are. Perhaps she kept her humiliation from him. Whatever the reason for his perplexity, Hannah needed more than Elkanah's soothing words. For the pain within, for the barrenness of her womb, she needed to hear from God.

❧

This went on year after year. Whenever Hannah went up to the house of the LORD, her rival [Peninnah] provoked her till she wept and would not eat.

Once when they had finished eating and drinking in Shiloh, Hannah stood up. Now Eli the priest was sitting on a chair by the doorpost of the LORD's temple. In bitterness of soul Hannah wept much and prayed to the LORD. And she made a vow, saying, "O LORD Almighty, if you will only look upon your servant's misery and remember me, and not forget your servant but give her a son, then I will give him to the LORD for all the days of his life, and no razor will ever be used on his head."

As she kept on praying to the LORD, Eli observed her mouth. Hannah was praying in her heart, and her lips were moving but her voice was not heard. Eli thought she was drunk and said to her, "How long will you keep on getting drunk? Get rid of your wine."

"Not so, my lord," Hannah replied, "I am a woman who is deeply troubled. I have not been drinking wine or beer; I was pouring out my soul to the LORD. Do not take your servant for a wicked woman; I have been praying here out of my great anguish and grief."

Eli answered, "Go in peace, and may the God of Israel grant you what you have asked of him."

She said, "May your servant find favor in your eyes."[1]

❦

When Hannah unlimbered her body from the temple floor, something had changed. Perhaps God had whispered in her ear. Perhaps Eli's blessing had been the Lord's words and they strengthened her.

Hannah did not say, but something within secured her heart. She ran back to the feast, cradled the meat in her hands, and thanked Elkanah for his generous helpings. She ate heartily, then looked into his astonished face and liberated her girlish laugh.

This is the Hannah I married, thought Elkanah. *This is the wife I want to carry home and embrace in nights of love.*

❦

Early the next morning they arose and worshiped before the LORD and then went back to their home at Ramah. Elkanah lay with Hannah his wife, and the LORD remembered her. So in the course of time Hannah conceived and gave birth to a son. She named him Samuel, saying, "Because I asked the LORD for him."

After he was weaned, she took the boy with her, young as he was, along with a three-year-old bull, an ephah of flour and a skin of wine, and brought him to the house of the LORD at Shiloh. When they had slaughtered the bull, they brought the boy to Eli, and she said to him, "As surely as you live, my lord, I am the woman who stood here beside you praying to the LORD. I prayed for this child, and the LORD has granted me what I asked of him. So now I give him to the LORD. For his whole life he will be given over to the LORD." And he worshiped the LORD there.

Then Elkanah went home to Ramah, but the boy ministered before the LORD under Eli the priest.[2]

The Inevitable Need

Into every woman's life there enters times when nothing but God's voice will do. Only His words will soothe her; only His promise can guide her. She may find consolation with loved ones; she might solicit advice from the experts. She may gather human wisdom and comfort and warnings, but no earthly communication can compare to the sound of His voice. Like Hannah lying prostrate in the temple, she pleads with God. Like Mary grieved and alone in the garden, she wants to cry "Rabboni!" when He gently speaks her name.

These are not the pleas of the demanding wife, the insatiable female. They are the cries of one who longs for the reassuring voice of her beloved. Like the lover in the Song of Songs, she sighs, "Show me your face, let me hear your voice" (2:14). She needs to hear from the person who will walk through the pain with her. It is a spontaneous and inevitable request, not because she is suffocatingly dependent but because the bonds of connection strengthen in crisis. When my sister learned of her son's terrible accident in another state, she immediately cried out for her husband. She needed the comfort of his presence but also the familiarity of his voice to assuage the pain.

The sound of a loved one's voice can calm the heart. Even in less dire or everyday circumstances this is true. "When I was a boy and sick in bed, the sound of my mother's voice in the kitchen comforted me and made me feel secure, even when I couldn't catch what she was saying," admitted my former pastor in a sermon. "These days when I am ill, I am comforted by the sound of my wife's voice in another room." We all need these touch points. When a family member returns from a trip, he calls out, "I'm home!" and expects a familiar voice to respond. When a friend rings my phone and says, "I just needed to hear your voice," we both feel nurtured.

Still, we need more than comfort from a familiar voice, as wonderful as those reassurances may be. From this person we also desire mutual guidance, partnership, enjoyment, trustworthiness, love. In our daily lives we want a steady stream of relationship with this individual. Then when a dam breaks, we can hear the familiar voice above the flood's roar. We already trust this person's faithfulness toward us and willingly listen to his or her advice. We do not need to get acquainted in the midst of difficulty.

So it is with God. When we are troubled, we need to hear His voice. We want the certainty of Isaiah's words: "Although the Lord gives you the bread of adversity and the water of affliction, your teachers will be hidden no more; with your own eyes you will see them. Whether you turn to the right or to the left, your ears will hear a voice behind you" (Isaiah 30:20–21). Yet we also crave daily fellowship with God, the intimate musings and everyday talks between the Father and His child. In the day-to-day decisions and directions, the routine chores and spontaneous joys, we want to hear His voice.

But how do we prompt God to speak to us?

I've wrestled with this question many times. On the one hand, I've learned I can't cajole or pressure the Creator into speaking to me. God is mighty and mysterious. He communicates to whomever He will, whenever and however He chooses to speak. He is not bound by human formulas, no matter how ardently we believe in them. Just when we think we've figured out His pattern, He does something that startles and proves us wrong —not because He is uncaring but because He is omnipotent and can't be predicted and controlled according to human logic.

Accordingly, God doesn't talk just to those who walk closely with Him. Scripture reveals that He speaks to both the righteous and unrighteous, the obedient and disobedient, the attentive and inattentive. If necessary, He'll use a donkey's mouth to get His message across (Numbers 22:28), but we cannot force Him to speak.

On the other hand, God the Father wants to speak to us. He is gracious and desirous of our companionship. He longs to spend time with His children—communing, comforting, leading, protecting—not out of duty but with delight. The Bible depicts Him as the Redeemer, continually reaching out to His beloved, always pursuing us with love. In turn, God's Word also claims that if we call, He will answer. "This is what the LORD says, he who made the earth, the LORD who formed it and established it—the LORD is his name: 'Call to me and I will answer you and tell you great and unsearchable things you do not know'" (Jeremiah 33:2–3). The Lord waits for our call, ever ready to answer. He wants us to know Him and His plans for us.

Consequently, a vital relationship with God holds these two perspectives in balance: understanding that God is not bound by our opinions about how and when He should speak but knowing He desires to talk with us. This is good news! The Almighty speaking to the lowly, not just dictating His messages but inviting the mutuality of two-way conversation. And though we can't box in His methods and timing, we can prepare our hearts to hear Him when He speaks. Like Hannah, we can become women searching for Jehovah's voice.

Shifting Our Desires

When I attended high school, my father periodically worked the late-night shift. I'd frequently go to bed before he arrived home from work and then leave for classes the next morning without seeing him. However, I did not forget he was the source for my lunch money and other financial quandaries. Nor did I waver on communicating with him about my empty billfold. At night I'd leave a note on the dining room table that explained my dilemma: "Dad, I need two dollars for lunch tomorrow." Or, "Could I have $10 to go to the football game?" The next morning the money appeared on the dining room table on top of my note.

It was a simple supply-and-demand relationship. No conversation, no listening to my father's thoughts, no intimacy. I loved my father deeply, but with teenage immaturity I expected Dad to answer my needs immediately without regard for what it cost him or for what he wanted. (My father only made a modest income, but he consistently produced the exact amount I requested.) Dad took seriously the responsibility to provide for his family, but now I wonder if he ever wanted to talk with me first—if he wanted to develop a relationship—instead of just plopping money on a table.

I'll never know. Dad died a few years later.

Looking back, I treasure my father's constancy toward me, but I also grieve the loss of relationship. Though I know Dad accepted my self-focus as part of the teenage years, and he didn't rebuke my attitude, I wish I'd understood that he had dreams and desires, too. I wish I'd asked him what those were. Tonight I'd love to greet him at the door and offer him a cup of decaf, along with the newspaper (his late-night ritual). But most of all I'd like to ask, "Dad, what do you want to tell me? What can I do for you?"

In a similar fashion it's possible not to mature beyond a self-centered relationship with the heavenly Father. In our prayers and longings we focus on our requests and eclipse knowing God and His thoughts. When we listen for His voice, we practice selective hearing, centering on what we want from Him rather than what He asks of us. We act as though God exists to serve us rather than our living to serve Him. The Scriptures encourage us to ask, seek, and knock (Matthew 7:7) but to ask according to His will and purpose in our lives (1 John 5:14). They also explain that we do not receive because we ask with wrong motives, "that [we] may spend what [we] get on [our] pleasures" (James 4:3). God gives us the desires of our hearts, but He asks that we delight in Him first (Psalm 37:4), and as we do so, we adopt His desires and alter our own.

Even if we're earnest about serving God, we can try using Him as a stamp of approval on our goals rather than listening to His plans for us. "We are a 'doing' people. We always want to be doing something," explains Henry T. Blackaby in his workbook *Experiencing God*. "I think God is crying out and shouting to us, 'Don't just do something. Stand there! Enter into a love relationship with Me. Get to know Me. Adjust your life to Me. Let Me love you and reveal Myself to you as I work through you.' A time will come when the doing will be called for, but we cannot skip the relationship. The relationship with God must come first."[3]

A relationship with God precedes our hearing from Him—a relationship in which we allow God to shift our desires. If we're willing to listen to what the Creator says rather than what we want to hear, if we're committed to knowing Him and His plans for us instead of demanding our own way, He will speak. God confides in the person with a "hearing heart."

Listening and Hearing

"We are talking, but you're not hearing what I say!"

More than once I've been told this by an exasperated friend. The first time someone accused me of conversing but not hearing I couldn't even grasp the concept. *What? Relating without hearing? How could that be?* But gradually as I've observed conversations, I've noticed my shabby listening skills. I've interrupted the speaker, barging in with my thoughts before she finishes hers. Or as she's talked, I've thought about what I want to say next, without truly listening. Or instead of focusing on her, I've continually referred back to my own needs and opinions. Or I've practiced all these annoyances at once, producing a friend's outburst.

Recognizing my inattentiveness and working on truly hearing hasn't been easy, but as I've made incremental progress, I've learned that blathering doesn't deepen a relationship. Hearing does.

When Christ's disciples weren't absorbing the truths He taught and modeled for them, He asked, "Do you have eyes but fail to see, and ears but fail to hear?" (Mark 8:18). He wanted them to open their ears and hearts so listening to Him would impact their lives.

James warned, "Do not merely listen to the word [of God], and so deceive yourselves. Do what it says. Anyone who listens to the word but does not do what it says is like a man who looks at his face in a mirror and, after looking at himself, goes away and immediately forgets what he looks like. But the man who looks intently into the perfect law that gives freedom, and continues to do this, not forgetting what he has heard, but doing it—he will be blessed in what he does" (James 1:22–25). When we hear God's voice, He asks the same "doing" of us.

But how do we cultivate a hearing heart? Hannah of the Old Testament reveals qualities we can emulate.

❦ *Searching.* I revel in the story of Hannah, drunk with urgent prayers, searching for God with an unquenchable thirst. She assures me that God rewards those who seek Him with all their hearts. The Bible says, "If...you seek the LORD your God, you will find him if you look for him with all your heart and with all your soul" (Deuteronomy 4:29). And, "You will seek me and find me when you seek me with all your heart. I will be found by you" (Jeremiah 29:13–14).

We search for God by praying, reading and meditating on His Word, participating in His Church, opening our eyes to His presence in everyday life, and in other ways unique to us. Whatever the method, when we wholeheartedly seek God, we will find Him, and finding Him, we can hear His voice. But first the question, *Are we willing to search?*

❦ *Believing.* Somewhere in her life Hannah heard about Jehovah and believed. She believed in God's promises and power to change lives. She believed in His desire to communicate with His people and answer their prayers. Most of all she believed in God's love and good-ness—that He gives good gifts to His children. Why else would she have been so persistent, so willing to prostrate herself in the temple, not caring about looking foolish?

The passage in Jeremiah that implores us to search for God adds this promise: "'For I know the plans I have for you,' declares the LORD, 'plans to prosper you and not to harm you, plans to give you hope and a future. Then you will call upon me and come and pray to me, and I will listen to you'" (29:11–12). When we search for God and find Him, we encounter a good Master, who speaks with love. Even if

He offers correction, we need not fear His voice. His motivations are good and beneficial to us.

Before Samuel was born, the omnipotent God had slated him to serve in the temple. Hannah would not give up on pregnancy because this generous Maker had dropped the desire into her heart. Centuries later the apostle James explained, "Every good and perfect gift is from above, coming down from the Father of the heavenly lights, who does not change like shifting shadows" (James 1:17). Understanding this, when we listen for God's voice, *do we believe in His goodness?*

❦ *Repenting.* Though I can't prove this with an exact verse, I believe Hannah moved from wanting a child for personal reasons to desiring God's purposes fulfilled through her. To repent means to "turn around," and Hannah initiated a radical, about-face move. Instead of clinging to the child-mother bond she craved, before Samuel's conception she offered him back to God for the priesthood. With trembling lips and tender heart she vowed, "O LORD Almighty, if you will only look upon your servant's misery and remember me, and not forget your servant but give her a son, then I will give him to the LORD for all the days of his life, and no razor will ever be used on his head" (1 Samuel 1:11).

Flawed and weary and wracked with pain, Hannah turned from her own way and handed the situation back to God. As soon as she did, the Bible says, "she went her way and ate something, and her face was no longer downcast" (verse 18). When Hannah changed her mind, it's possible God spoke to her at this point, for her spirit lightened, and she left the temple at peace. It's not evident what happened between the

27

vow and her departure, but it's apparent that when Hannah loosened her grip, she received from God.

With a similar mind-set, we may need to repent of sins, desires, attitudes, and motivations or merely change our way of thinking before we can hear God's voice. We need to ask, *Are we willing to repent?*

❦ *Waiting.* "I wait for you, O LORD; you will answer, O Lord my God," wrote David (Psalm 38:15), who spent many years of his life waiting for divine interventions. It's possible David learned about waiting for God's voice from Samuel, who anointed him for kingship. Maybe in a conversation with the young shepherd, the old priest reminisced about his mother, Hannah, who learned to wait on God for what felt like an eternity. The connection of Hannah to Samuel to David is fascinating, and in our own lives, learning to wait could yield equally intriguing associations. We don't know what creative surprises God holds in store. We're just told to wait.

As perplexing as it can be, God doesn't speak on our timetable, and His ways are inscrutable. Still, if we belong to God, we need to hear His voice for direction. If we act with God's guidance, the outcome can be powerful. (Remember David and Goliath.) If we act apart from Him, we create disasters. (Also remember David and Bathsheba.) So if we need to hear God's voice, *are we willing to wait?*

❦ *Obeying.* When Samuel was born, Hannah didn't forget her promise to God. Though it wrenched the mother's soul to relinquish her boy, to place his chubby hand in Eli's and walk away, she kept her vow. No matter the cost. In essence, this is obedience. We make a commitment to God and follow through on it. When we hear from

Him, we do what He says. Jesus said, "Blessed rather are those who hear the word of God and obey it" (Luke 11:28). So counting the cost, *are we willing to obey?*

In 1915 during the Great War, a young Scotsman stood in his friend's kitchen, ready to say good-bye. "I am going out to Egypt to help the men in the armed forces," said the athletic-looking Oswald Chambers. "I have a Bible text: 'I am now ready to be offered' (2 Timothy 4:6). I do not know what it means, but I am ready."4

This is how Oswald Chambers approached his spiritual life and calling. He didn't need to understand everything God wanted from him; it only mattered that he unswervingly followed the Lord. This attitude of obedience led him from an artistic career into the ministry, first as an itinerant evangelist, then as a Bible college teacher, and finally as a spiritual shepherd to troops at war in Egypt.

Years before, Oswald had written: "I feel I shall be buried for a time, hidden away in obscurity; then suddenly I shall flame out, do my work and be gone." His instincts proved true. While in Egypt the revered teacher fell ill quickly and died at age forty-three.

From a physical viewpoint God cut short His servant's life, but from a spiritual perspective the obedient Scot still deeply affects lives today. Eighty years after his death, Oswald's teachings thrive through many books based on his wife Gertrude's shorthand notes of his sermons. In addition, his perennial devotional, *My Utmost for His Highest,* has sold millions of copies and ranks among the world's classics.

Such popularity would have surprised and embarrassed Oswald, who never intended for his works to be published. He only wanted to hear and obey God.

This, too, is the desire of the hearing heart. Not to seek its own purposes, not to pursue human adulation, but to find and follow the divine agenda.

Chapter Two

The Divine Agenda

So what must we do? To begin with, we must hear His voice.
Sometimes we hear His voice through the prickings of the conscience,
sometimes through the gropings of the mind... by which we
become aware that Christ is outside the door and speaking to us.
Or his call can come to us through a friend, a preacher, or a book.
Whenever we hear, we must listen.
"He who has ears to hear," Jesus says, "let him hear."

JOHN R. W. STOTT

I do not think grandly when I wake in the morning. Usually I focus on two routine duties, both motivated by necessity. The first is *I have to go to the bathroom.* The second: *I have to feed the cat.* Until I navigate these urgencies, my mind stays in neutral, so I felt startled one morning to wake up to an unexpected agenda. As soon as I opened my eyes, the plan for a specialized writers' retreat presented itself, sitting on my brain as if it'd been waiting for me to stir.

How strange, I thought. *Where did this come from?* I hadn't been musing on the idea the night before or for that matter aspiring to start new projects. I had a book to write and that felt like enough. Still groggy with sleep, I rolled to the bed's other side, only to be greeted with specific instructions. *Start up a weekend retreat for women,* said the voice in my head. *But not just any women. It must be for women who want to minister through the written word. The ones who'd be serious about it. Hand select the participants from women you already know, and pour your knowledge into them. Teach them about the writing life. Prepare them for influence.*

I rolled back again, pondering the possibility. *This might be God,* I thought. *I wouldn't have considered this, especially not the first thing in the morning.* Besides, the idea made sense. In the past few years at out-of-town retreats and conferences I'd met women who'd confided they felt called to write but didn't know how to begin. My spirit resonated with their desire to publish, yet given the circumstances, I could only offer them a few encouraging insights. But bringing them to my town for a retreat? That might work.

By the time I fired up the coffeemaker, the idea captivated me, and I breathed a hesitant prayer. *Okay, God, I'll make a list and write letters,* I told Him, dropping a little toe into the waters of faith. *But I don't have money to invest in this, and these women are very busy leading their own ministries and raising families. It seems impossible they'd all have the same weekend open. If this really is from You, they'll be available and say yes.*

Several days later I devised a rough budget for the weekend, including food, lodging, transportation, and materials, and gave God my financial criteria, as if He didn't already know my needs. *Lord, if this is from You,* I said, silently repeating my uncertainty, *then I'll need at least ten women who can pay enough to cover the expenses.*

Plan it for the first weekend in October, came the reply.

A few weeks later, after the idea burrowed deeper into my heart, I sent an invitation letter to fifteen women. Would they be interested? Or would they laugh? I'd soon find out. However, instead of dictating a date, I asked the women to vote for which of four weekends in September and October would best fit their schedules. In the next month ten women replied with a yes, and when I tallied their preferences, they all had the same time slot open: the first weekend in October. I knew I had to quit second-guessing God, follow instructions, and start moving.

≥

Over the next few months the participants increased to twelve and the retreat fell into place in a way I'd never experienced before. (I'm accustomed to wrestling project details to the ground, but for this event the particulars embraced me.) Women volunteered to help facilitate the weekend, two of my publishers made financial contributions, men and women covenanted to pray for individual participants and their needs—the list goes on. During my research for a book project, a name emerged for the gathering: The Vision Group, based on the Habakkuk verse, "Write the vision, and make it plain upon tables, that he may run that readeth it" (2:2, KJV). I'd heard that when God initiates a project it flows in ways we'd never manage on our own. The retreat was becoming living proof. The Lord knew what He was doing; I only had to follow and watch Him perform.

A few weeks before the retreat, as I considered what I'd teach the group about writing, another unexpected instruction walked across my mind. *Be willing to set aside your agenda and follow Mine.* Now this felt more challenging. I'd taught many writing classes, and good or bad, my teaching style crammed in as much information as possible, complete with handouts to take home. *Set aside my notes and wing it?* Already I was concerned about not having enough time for all the necessary information. *What would we do?*

Based on God's performance so far, I decided to trust Him with this directive, too, though I'd never taught by the wing-it method before. Curiously, I wasn't the only one wondering about the weekend. Several participants had sent notes that admitted, "I don't know why I'm coming to this. I just know God told me to come." At least we'd all be clueless together.

That weekend I learned if we're obedient to God's voice, it's all right not to understand everything He plans to do. In fact, it's an advantage to be uninformed; it makes us flexible and reliant upon Him. Or in my case, slightly uneasy. I didn't know how to lead an entire weekend without being in control of every session.

❧

True to His word, God intruded on the first teaching session. As I talked about the characteristics of writers, I asked, "As a child, alone in your room, did you write?" Frequently this indicates a writer has been born. A few minutes later two women interrupted me, one after the other, to say they'd just flashed back to a long-forgotten childhood incident. In each case the woman wrote something meaningful to her, but an insensitive family member ridiculed her writing. Both felt that without realizing it, the ridicule materialized as a fear that blocked them from writing as adults. Soon after this revelation, during break time a few participants prayed for these women, asking God to release them from fear.

Amazing, I thought. *God, what else will You do this weekend?* It didn't take long to find out. That session set the pattern, and for three days I rearranged my lectures to make room for ministry. Collectively we confronted other fears about writing, prayed for physical ailments that hinder the creative process, counseled and interceded for women with emotional wounds, sought God for direction in each woman's life, listened to His words to us, and drank in His vision and renewal. Revealing the specifics would break confidences, and I don't know everything God accomplished when women formed friendships, talked in their hotel rooms at night, strolled around the premises, or huddled in small prayer or discussion groups. I don't need to know. Watching God work was plenty.

However, I understand this: Last October God called some women to write and touched them in deep and profound ways. During that time participants repeatedly thanked me for the retreat, and I could only say, "Thank God. It was His idea." I wasn't conjuring up false humility, merely telling the truth. When God acts on His agenda, it's impossible for humans to take the credit.

God, the Great Initiator

When God wants to communicate, He is the Great Initiator. He even has a flair for the dramatic. Certainly this was true in the Scriptures. He spoke to Moses through a burning bush. He drenched a fleece to transform Gideon from a timid farmer into a mighty warrior. He cast three young Hebrews into a blasting furnace, where they confidently stood, unsinged, to capture the attention of an arrogant king. He delivered a birth announcement to Mary via an angel. He temporarily blinded Saul to liberate his Pharisaical soul and call him to missionary work. He swept the apostle John to heaven in a vision, revealing mysteries of the future.

Yet despite His penchant for the spectacular, God also initiated communication through common people and events. He influenced Ruth by her and Naomi's grief-filled circumstances. He challenged Esther through the voice of a relative. He drew Timothy to Himself with a mother's and grandmother's instruction. Still, these ordinary channels contributed to the miraculous. Whenever and however God spoke, He talked of spiritual redemption.

God still employs a variety of communication methods today, but however He speaks, the underlying message remains steadfastly the same. Thousands of years after God spoke to Abraham about many descendants, pointing the patriarch to a star-littered sky, He still speaks about redemption. He woos us to salvation and redeems our souls from eternal death. He pursues conforming us into Christ's image, redeeming us from barriers to spiritual change and growth. He asks us to participate in bringing others to redemption so together we can stride into heaven.

The prophet Isaiah described the final destination of God's redeemed ones: "And a highway will be there; it will be called the Way of Holiness. The unclean will not journey on it; it will be for those who walk in that Way; wicked fools will not go about on it. No lion will be there, nor will any ferocious beast get up on it; they will not be found there. But only the redeemed will walk there, and the ransomed of the LORD will return. They will enter Zion with singing; everlasting joy will crown their heads. Gladness and joy will overtake them, and sorrow and sighing will flee away" (Isaiah 35:8–10).

This is the divine agenda: to redeem us on earth for the joys of Zion. This is what compels the Creator to initiate communication with us. God is love, and He does not want anyone to perish, but longs for everyone to come to repentance (2 Peter 3:9). Redemption underscores all of His communication, all of His plans, though the specifics vary from person to person and situation to situation. Understanding this principle can revolutionize our relationship with God. Instead of viewing Him as someone we badger into speaking, we gradually awaken to the fact He is a passionate, frequent communicator. We can spend less time talking about ourselves and more time listening for His redemptive messages. We can ask, "What is God initiating?" rather than "Why doesn't He talk when I want Him to?"

"To live a God-centered life you must focus on God's purposes, not your own plans. You must seek from God's perspective rather than from your own distorted human perspective," explains author Henry Blackaby. "When God starts to do something in the world, He takes the initiative to come and talk to somebody. For some divine reason,

He has chosen to involve His people in accomplishing His purposes."[1] When we walk intimately with God, He speaks to us about how to participate with Him. When we put His priorities first, we then dis-cover Him responding to our needs. Jesus said, "But seek first *his kingdom* and *his righteousness,* and all these things will be given to you as well" (Matthew 6:33, author's italics). This includes our desire to hear from God.

But what, in particular, does God say to us? Though the follow-ing lists are not comprehensive (who can limit God?), with Scriptures and stories they exemplify a variety of His redemptive messages.

Expressions of Love and Relationship

After God hands us His gift of salvation, He continues to cultivate a redemptive relationship with us. His first priority is one-to-one interaction with His children.

❧ *He expresses His love.* "I have loved you with an everlasting love; I have drawn you with loving-kindness" (Jeremiah 31:3). There is no limit to God's love or the ways He expresses it to us, and often He asks us to speak His love to others.

"I will tell you something that happened when I was a prisoner in a [Nazi] concentration camp with my sister Betsie," announced the Dutch woman Corrie ten Boom to a young person she counseled. "One morning I had a terrible cold and I said to Betsie, 'What can I do? I have no handkerchief.'

"'Pray,' she said. I smiled, but she prayed, 'Father, Corrie has got a cold, and she has no handkerchief. Will You give her one? In Jesus' name, Amen.' I could not help but laugh. As she said, 'Amen,' I heard my name called. I went to the window, and there stood my friend who worked in the prison hospital.

"'Quickly, quickly! Take this little package,' and inside was a handkerchief.

"'Why in the world did you bring me this? Did I ask you for it? Did you know that I have a cold?'

"'No, but I was folding handkerchiefs in the hospital, and a voice in my heart said, *Take one to Corrie ten Boom.*'

"What a miracle! Can you understand what that handkerchief told me at that moment? It told me that in heaven there is a loving Father."[2]

❦ *He declares His presence.* "My eyes will watch over them for their good, and I will bring them back to this land. I will build them up and not tear them down; I will plant them and not uproot them" (Jeremiah 24:6). God may declare His presence to say, "I am here," or "I am pleased with you," or "I'm not letting go of you."

After years of spiritual rebellion in my twenties I unexpectedly returned to God. At the end of a day sailing with a boyfriend, I entered my living room alone, settled on the couch, and said, "God, I'm giving my life back to You."

The statement shocked me; it felt like someone else had said it. In an instant God responded, not allowing me to change my mind. The Holy Spirit rushed in, flooding me with joy and peace. I laughed, praised God, and wondered, *Now where in the world did I hide my Bible?*

Fifteen years later I still don't know why I returned to God at that moment, but I do remember the lasting impression of His presence.

❦ *He comforts the soul.* "I, even I, am he who comforts you" (Isaiah 51:12). Often God speaks His comfort to us through the Bible, the words of consoling people, the certainty of His presence, or supernatural intervention.

A middle-aged man described God's comfort as a newfound strength. He explained, "I left work early after hearing that I would lose my job. I got in my car and went to my church. Unfortunately the minister was not there. But the chapel was open. I went in and stared at the cross. I started to cry. I told God that I didn't have the strength to get through this mess. And I asked for help. I must have stayed there for a couple of hours. I brushed away the tears. Suddenly a whole load went off my shoulders. I can't explain it, but I went into that chapel crushed. And I came out feeling strong."[3]

The Voice of Guidance and Insight

God also guides us through life's details and decisions, dangers and disappointments. He wants us to understand that we're not alone and that He's in control, even if the circumstances feel uncertain.

❦ *He answers prayer.* "He will call upon me, and I will answer him; I will be with him in trouble, I will deliver him and honor him" (Psalm 91:15). The Lord answers our prayers not only when we're in trouble but in everyday situations too. Whether He says yes, no, wait, or "I have a better way to do it," He wants to "answer you and tell you great and unsearchable things you do not know" (Jeremiah 33:3).

About a month ago I hit a financial low in my business, and emotionally and practically I felt like giving up. One morning while soaking in the bathtub (God hears our prayers anywhere!), I asked, "Lord, is this worth it? Do the books I write affect lives? Do You really want me to continue?" God didn't ripple the waters or speak to my heart, so I considered the questions rhetorical and pushed into the day.

The next morning a woman from Canada called me.

"Are you the Judith Couchman who writes books?" she asked.

"Yes, this is Judy," I answered, feeling on guard.

She started to cry. "I read one of your books, and it's changed my life," she said. "I want to thank you—and tell you that you're making a difference out there." As she poured out her story, I blinked back tears too. She was God's voice to me.

❦ *He asks us to pray.* "Then Jesus told his disciples a parable to show them that they should always pray and not give up" (Luke 18:1). God quickens us to pray for people and situations, even if we're uninformed about the details.

My pastor tells this story about praying for a situation he didn't fully understand: "One morning several years ago as I was praying, the Lord gave me a mental picture. Some might call it a vision. Whatever it is called, I saw something: a rattlesnake coiled at my dad's feet.... I spent about fifteen minutes praying earnestly for his protection until I felt released from the urgency.

"The next day he called me—he was in Florida, I was in Texas—and said, "'You'll never guess what happened yesterday. Jodie (my stepmother) went out back to the shed. Before walking in as she normally would, she pushed the door open, stopped, and looked down. There where she was about to step was a coiled rattlesnake. She backed away carefully, came and got me, and I killed it.'"[4]

❦ *He calls us to servanthood.* "I took you from the ends of the earth, from its farthest corners I called you. I said, 'You are my servant'; I have chosen you and have not rejected you" (Isaiah 41:9). Whether it's a lifetime call or a single task, God asks us to be His servants. He may reveal our mission gradually over time or all at once.

My friend Anne recently bought a country living store, and the transition in ownership has proved challenging and sometimes overwhelming. She's been under so much stress, I've fussed about the dangers to her health. Anne's employees are caring and competent, but she's also needed a personal assistant who could lift the load both at home and work.

"You need somebody like Aaron who held up Moses' arms as the Israelites battled the Amalekites," I told her wistfully. Anne agreed. But who would it be? There was no time to look for someone, so she shelved the idea.

Not long after this conversation Anne received a phone call from Marilyn, a friend who lives in another state.

"Anne, God kept putting your name in my mind," said Marilyn. "Do you need help? I think He is asking me to come and help you."

Because of cutbacks, Marilyn had lost her job with a Christian organization, and instead of finding another position, she'd accepted God's call to assist people in need as He led her to them. Marilyn had just completed a six-month stay with a friend who's battling cancer when Anne's name kept coming to mind. The result: Marilyn is now functioning as Anne's assistant—working at the store but also cooking and cleaning and lifting the load at home. The arrangement will last for at least six weeks, helping Anne through a pressured season. Marilyn has humbled us all with her availability to God's voice and the tasks He assigns her.

❧ *He gives insight and wisdom.* "Praise be to the name of God for ever and ever; wisdom and power are his. He changes times and seasons; he sets up kings and deposes them. He gives wisdom to the wise and knowledge to the discerning. He reveals deep and hidden things; he knows what lies in darkness, and light dwells with him" (Daniel 2:20–22). In perplexing situations when we can't uncover a problem's source, God can grant a deeper understanding.

For a while I worked with a man who disliked women. He constantly felt ill at ease around women in meetings, and business lunches with female colleagues were anathema to him, and he told me so. The attitude created undercurrents of disunity in our department, but I didn't know what to do about it. He also fought against me, his manager. Then unexpectedly I discovered that this employee struggled with pornography, and his attitude, though still not acceptable, made sense to me. I didn't just have an unhappy employee; I was caught in a spiritual battle.

❧ *He guides our steps.* "I will lead the blind by ways they have not known, along unfamiliar paths I will guide them; I will turn the darkness into light before them and make the rough places smooth.

These are the things I will do; I will not forsake them" (Isaiah 42:16). God gives direction, changes our course, and guides even when we feel in the dark about what to do. Often when we think He's doing nothing to help us, the Lord is working in the blackness to shed light on our paths. Sometimes He interrupts our comfortable surroundings or cherished goals with a new destiny.

Last night I attended a dinner for newcomers at my church. After the meal participants introduced themselves and explained why they had chosen this congregation as a church home. Person after person, story after story pointed to a God who directs our steps. One couple said, "God told each of us separately that we were going to Colorado Springs." Another man explained, "I was sitting in my recliner, watching television, and God said, 'I'm taking you to a new place.'"

Many spoke of needing a safe place to heal after burnout or stressful ministry positions or emotional wounds. Without question, this church is a haven, and across the world God guides people to its doors—to minister and to be ministered to when they're weary.

❦ *He instills courage.* "So do not fear, for I am with you; do not be dismayed, for I am your God. I will strengthen you and help you; I will uphold you with my righteous right hand" (Isaiah 41:10). God can fill us with courage for the personal challenges and spiritual battles now and in the future.

A few years ago the mother of my friend Kathe paid her a surprise birthday visit. "Kathe, God prompted me to come to see you," explained her mother one evening. "For some reason I believe you need encouragement. That's what I want to give you for your birthday—*words* to give you hope and courage." She then told her daughter about the women in their heritage who begged God to give them children and sometimes lost the babies they bore but never gave up on faith in God.

Later, after fifteen years of marriage and infertility, and consequently adopting a son, Kathe became pregnant. Several months into the pregnancy, however, an ultrasound delivered devastating news. "Your baby has no chance of survival," said the doctor.

Despite the prognosis Kathe determined to carry the baby full term. "God continued to use Mom's 'faith stories' to give me hope and courage during the long months of waiting for the birth of my baby," she explained. Her son, John Samuel, died a few hours after his birth. Despite the horrible loss, Kathe still believes God spoke to her through those stories, preparing her for the year ahead. For this she is grateful and says, "God turned fear into confident faith."

❦ *He prompts good works.* "For we are God's workmanship, created in Christ Jesus to do good works, which God prepared in advance for us to do" (Ephesians 2:10). God uses us to be His mouthpiece to others, and often we can express His love and attention through what the Bible calls "good works." These works comprise acts of service, devotion, and kindness to believers and nonbelievers.

I'd been invited to dinner at a single mom's house, and the offer touched me. I knew Elaine didn't have much money, but she wanted to share from her modest supply. What an honor; what an expression of purely motivated giving!

On the way to Elaine's I stopped at the grocery store, and while walking to the checkout counter, the words *flowers* and *bubble gum* popped into my mind. *That's weird,* I thought. *Why would I suddenly think of these items?* I debated for a few moments. *Could this be God's voice telling me something? Am I supposed to take flowers and bubble gum to my friend's home?*

Finally I decided, *No, it can't be.* I didn't think the message was mystical enough to be from God. Certainly He wouldn't sound so concise and practical, and I doubted He'd involve Himself with such minutiae. I left the grocery store and soon entered my friend's house empty-handed.

During our conversation that evening I mentioned my strange message, and Elaine looked astonished. "Wow, my favorite gift is fresh flowers, and my son absolutely loves bubble gum," she said gently. I felt stunned. It had been God talking to me, prompting me toward a small but good work.

❦ *He reveals the future.* "For the vision is yet for an appointed time, but at the end it shall speak, and not lie: though it tarry, wait for it; because it will surely come, it will not tarry" (Habakkuk 2:3, KJV). Whether the vision is global or personal, God occasionally unfolds the future to His children. Sometimes He speaks in generalities, other times with detail, about future events in individual lives or the Body of Christ.

For several years when I worked as an editor, I traveled to writers conferences to teach and consult with aspiring writers. One afternoon a young woman approached me and said, "I have a word for you from God."

"Oh, yeah?" I said, blinking back my disbelief.

"Yes," she said. The gist of the message was, "God wants you to know that you're called to a ministry in writing and teaching. But to do this, you'll need supporters, and they will gather around you to help you. You've also had much pain in your life, but it will be healed. You are valuable like gold in God's eyes, and He's refining you for the ministry ahead."

"Thank you," I said, humbled but wondering if I dared believe it.

That was twelve years ago. Since then, what she said has come true.

❦ *He warns about oppressors.* "Watch out for false prophets. They come to you in sheep's clothing, but inwardly they are ferocious wolves. By their fruit you will recognize them" (Matthew 7:15–16). Through a specific warning or a sense of unease, God warns us about the "sheep in wolves' clothing" we encounter.

A friend of mine recently attended a prayer retreat. As she read the Scriptures that weekend, she kept encountering verses about untrustworthy people. She felt God was warning her about someone but wasn't sure of the details. It didn't take long to find out. In the next few weeks she uncovered that an insecure employee was gossiping about her to vendors, trying to ruin her business. Armed with the assurance of her warning verses, she then watched God banish the employee from the job and repair the verbal damage.

The Voice of Conviction and Correction

If we stray from God and His principles for living, He speaks up. He wants to draw us back to the everlasting way. But even while we're pursuing His path, He teaches and steadies us when we falter.

❦ *He convicts the wayward.* "If my people, who are called by my name, will humble themselves and pray and seek my face and turn from their wicked ways, then will I hear from heaven and will forgive their sin and will heal their land" (2 Chronicles 7:14). Like a jealous lover, the Lord pursues us continually, pulling us back into His arms if we're wayward. Though He's granted us the freedom to choose our direction, He wants to redeem and walk with us. Thankfully, He doesn't like taking no for an answer and sometimes resorts to extreme measures to bring us back.

A former drug addict explained God's pursuit of him in a letter he wrote from jail to the people who'd been praying for him. He explained, "After I got arrested with multiple felony charges, I had no idea how drastically and quickly God would do His work. Before my arrest, my life was selling drugs. I was indifferent to my family and wasting my education. God rescued me from the depth of my despair by raiding my apartment and instantly cleaning out the physical impurities of my life. From that point God took care of me and began to work in my life. He let me out of jail, even though my bail was set at $50,000, brought me home to a spiritual family and friends, and gave me only six months in jail when I could have had years in prison."

He added, "Jail was the most awesome time of my life. I had the privilege to leave this world and my old life and hang out with God for four months. He turned me completely inside out, and I learned and experienced the strength of His perspective. My life is now His, and I cannot wait to see what He does with it."[5]

❦ *He corrects our attitudes.* "The heart is deceitful above all things and beyond cure. Who can understand it? I the LORD search the heart and examine the mind, to reward a man according to his conduct, according to what his deeds deserve" (Jeremiah 17:9–10). God reaches into our hearts and sweeps out the sinful attitudes that clutter our thinking and thwart the ability to minister His truth to the world effectively.

Once while sitting in my car at the gas station, waiting for a fill-up, I watched a dirty, raggedy man hobble along the sidewalk. He looked intoxicated, and I sized him up as a loser. Then a question startled my thoughts: *What makes you think you're any better than that man?*

It didn't take long to figure out the message. Life hadn't been going my way, and I'd blamed God for it. So with a few pointed words, He challenged my demanding attitude: the belief that I was entitled to more than anyone else. God wanted me to know that He loves everyone equally and that my attitude needed an adjustment.

❦ *He teaches us to persevere.* "As long as it is day, we must do the work of him who sent me. Night is coming, when no one can work" (John 9:4). We're not only to persevere in short-term, God-given assignments but also in the spiritual long haul. With the Holy Spirit's power and guidance, we can walk with God for a lifetime.

I'll never forget when I received my first freelance writing assignment. Excited and nervous, I took the project seriously and wanted inspiration from God before beginning.

That weekend I baby-sat a friend's dog and began work on the long-awaited assignment. However, I didn't have an idea for the piece, so I decided to pray about it first. I paced back and forth in the house, the dog alongside, asking God to bless my work and to give me a good idea. Then I dropped to the floor and prayed with my face down. The dog plopped on the floor beside me.

"Oh, God, please give me Your idea for writing this project," I prayed for the umpteenth time. The dog whined. That's when I heard the answer; it wasn't what I expected.

Get up and get to work, He said.

In a few words God pinpointed my problem. I'd given a fine spiritual performance, but truthfully, I was procrastinating. God gave me the push I needed to get started.

I used to think God spoke only to the "super Christians," the ones with special dispensations from Him or the ones who devoted their lives to contemplation. But as I've experienced and observed God at work in "ordinary" people's lives, I've learned He speaks to all of His children, if they're willing to listen. Like the everyday people in these pages, they can discern the sound of His voice.

"God talks to us. It is a wonder that He would have something to say to us and a deeper wonder still that He would want to talk to us. And that from deep within Him would come all the messages He has been wanting to tell us," wrote the author Bob Benson.[6] We can begin receiving these messages by exploring the Scriptures, the Word He's already spoken to us all.

Chapter Three

The Word Already Spoken

Words written fifty years ago, a hundred years ago,
a thousand years ago, can have as much...power today
as ever they had it then to come alive for us and in us
and to make us more alive within ourselves.
That, I suppose, is the final mystery as well as the final power of words:
that not even across great distances of time and space do they
ever lose their capacity for becoming incarnate.

FREDERICK BUECHNER

Christian was walking in the fields reading his book, and greatly distressed in his mind; and as he read, he burst out, as he had done before, crying, "What shall I do to be saved?"

He looked this way and that way, as if he would run; yet he stood still, because he could not tell which way to go.

A man named Evangelist came to him, and asked, "Wherefore dost thou cry?"

He answered, "Sir, I perceive by the book in my hand that I am condemned to die, and after that to come to judgment, and I find that I am not willing to do the first, nor able to do the second."

Then said Evangelist, "Why not willing to die, since this life is attended with so many evils?"

The man answered, "Because I fear that this burden that is upon my back will sink me lower than the grave, and I shall fall into Tophet. And, sir, if I be not fit to go to prison, I am not fit to go to judgment, and from thence to execution; and the thoughts of these things make me cry."

Then said Evangelist, "If this be thy condition, why standest thou still?"

He answered, "Because I know not whither to go."

Then Evangelist gave him a parchment roll, and there was written within, "Fly from the wrath to come."

The man therefore read it, and looking upon Evangelist very carefully, said, "Whither must I fly?"

Then said Evangelist, pointing with his finger over a very wide field, "Do you see yonder wicket-gate?"

The man said, "No."

Then said the other, "Do you see yonder shining light?"

He said, "I think I do."

Then said Evangelist, "Keep that light in your eye, and go up directly thereto: so shalt thou see the gate; at which when thou knockest it shall be told thee what thou shalt do."

So he looked not behind him, but fled towards the middle of the plain....

❧

The neighbours came to see him run; and as he ran, some mocked, others threatened, and some cried after him to return; and, among those that did so, there were two that resolved to fetch him back by force. The name of the one was Obstinate, and the name of the other Pliable. Now by this time the man was a good distance from them; but, however, they were resolved to pursue him, which they did, and in a little time they overtook him.

Then said the man, "Neighbours, wherefore are ye come?"

They said, "To persuade you to go back with us."

But he said, "That can by no means be; you dwell in the City of Destruction, the place also where I was born: I see it to be so; and dying there, sooner or later, you will sink lower than the grave, into a place that burns with fire and brimstone: be content, good neighbours, and go along with me."

"What!" said Obstinate, "and leave our friends and our comforts behind us?"

"Yes," said Christian, "because all that which you shall forsake is not worthy to be compared with a little of that which I am seeking to enjoy; and if you will go along with me,....you shall fare as I myself; for there where I go is enough and to spare. Come away, and prove my words."

"What are the things you seek, since you leave all the world to find them?" asked Obstinate.

"I seek 'an inheritance incorruptible, undefiled, and that fadeth not away,' and it is laid up in heaven, and safe there, to be bestowed, at the time appointed, on them that diligently seek it. Read it so, if you will, in my book."

"Tush," said Obstinate, "away with your book. Will you go back with us or no?"

"No, not I," said the other, "because I have laid my hands to the plough."

"Come then, neighbour Pliable, let us turn again and go home without him," said Obstinate. "There is a company of these crazed-headed coxcombs, that, when they take a fancy by the end, are wiser in their own eyes 'than seven men that can render a reason.'"

Then said Pliable, "Don't revile; if what the good Christian says is true, the things he looks after are better than ours; my heart inclines to go with my neighbour."

"What! More fools still," cried Obstinate. "Be ruled by me, and go back; who knows whither such a brain-sick fellow will lead you? Go back, go back, and be wise."

"Nay," said Christian, "but do thou come with thy neighbour, Pliable; there are such things to be had which I spoke of, and many more glories besides. If you believe not me, read here in this book; and for the truth of what is expressed therein, behold all is confirmed by the blood of Him that made it."

"Well, neighbour Obstinate," said Pliable, "I begin to come to a point; I intend to go along with this good man, and to cast in my lot with him; but, my good companion, do you know the way to this desired place?"

Christian replied, "I am directed by a man whose name is Evangelist, to speed me to a little gate that is before us, where we shall receive instructions about the way."

"Come then, good neighbour, let us be going," said Pliable. Then they went both together.

"And I will go back to my place," said Obstinate. "I will be no companion of such misled, fantastical fellows."

When Obstinate was gone back, Christian and Pliable went talk-ing over the plain; and thus they began their discourse.

※

"Come, neighbour Pliable, how do you do?" asked Christian. "I am glad you are persuaded to go along with me. Had even Obstinate him-self but felt what I have felt of the power and terrors of what is yet unseen, he would not thus lightly have given us the back."

Pliable answered, "Come, neighbour Christian, since there are none but us two here, tell me now further what the things are, and how to be enjoyed, whither we are going."

"I can better conceive of them with my mind, than speak of them with my tongue, but yet, since you are desirous to know, I will read of them in my book," said Christian.

"And do you think the words of your book are certainly true?"

"Yes, verily; for it was made by Him that cannot lie."[1]

The Life-Shaking Book

In the opening of *The Pilgrim's Progress*, the character Christian reads the Book, and it so shakes him he leaves family, friends, and community to pursue its promise of everlasting life. Such is the power of God's Word. When it leaps into our path, it demands a response. We can dodge or outright reject it. We can doubt its truth and stall our reply. We can flip through its pages apathetically. But when we accept the Word wholeheartedly, it profoundly changes our lives.

Paul told us, "the word of God is living and active. Sharper than any double-edged sword, it penetrates even to dividing soul and spirit, joints and marrow; it judges the thoughts and attitudes of the heart" (Hebrews 4:12). When we accept Christ as Savior, this sword slashes through the night and by its gleaming blade leads us into the light. The Word severs our desire for the world and replaces it with Christ. In fact, everything about the Bible feels radical and compelling, and following its guidance, our lives are quickly revolutionized, drawing a line of demarcation between us and evil.

When my friend Marcia became a Christian, she spent hours reading the Bible, after a full day working at the office and corralling children at home. Whatever she read there, she obeyed. Within months she stopped swearing, broke off an affair, started attending church, reordered her finances, quit smoking and drinking, learned intercessory prayer, and sought people's forgiveness. Marcia stepped out of the world, and with Bible in tow, she didn't look back. It was whirlwind change. But no wonder: Coming to salvation can be our initial experience of hearing God through His Word, and He beckons us with a shout. We are in life-and-death circumstances, and He wants us to choose life.

However, once we choose life, we need to learn how to live. We begin the process of sanctification—being transformed into Christ's image—and the scenario changes again. The apologist C. S. Lewis explained, "When a man turns to Christ, and seems to be getting on pretty well (in the sense that some of his bad habits are being corrected), he often feels that it would now be natural if things went fairly smoothly. When troubles come along—illnesses, money troubles, new kinds of temptations—he is disappointed. These things, he feels, might have been necessary to rouse him and make him repent in his bad old days; but why now? Because God is forcing him on, or up, to a higher level: putting him into situations where he will have to be very much braver, or more patient, than he ever dreamed of being before. It seems to us all unnecessary: but that is because we have not yet had the slightest notion of the tremendous thing He seems to make of us.... The command *Be ye perfect* [Matthew 5:48] is no idealistic gas. Nor is it a command to do the impossible. He is going to make us into creatures that can obey that command."[2]

Psalm 18:30 says, "As for God, his way is perfect; the word of the LORD is flawless," and we need the Bible's purity to lead us into perfection. "No possible degree of holiness or heroism which has ever been recorded of the greatest saints is beyond what He is determined to produce in every one of us in the end," said Lewis. "The job will not be completed in this life, but He means to get us as far as possible before death."[3] To this end, God continues to speaks to us through His Word, usually with a quiet, steady voice.

The Word at Face Value

Christians through the ages have heard God's voice through the Scriptures, both corporately and individually, and these printed words are still His courier today. We can read and study the Bible to understand God's opinion on many issues, but to do so, there are foundational principles we need to accept about the surety of His Word. These principles emerge from what God says about Himself and Scripture, and He expects us to accept His Word "at face value."

If we don't embrace these facts, we'll tend to disbelieve the validity of the Bible's words to us personally, either dismissing Scriptures or second-guessing them. If we accept them, we'll learn to trust and rest in the Scriptures as our guide.

❦ *The Bible is God's Word.* Paul wrote, "We did not follow cleverly invented stories when we told you about the power and coming of our Lord Jesus Christ, but we were eyewitnesses of his majesty.... Above all, you must understand that no prophecy of Scripture came about by the prophet's own interpretation. For prophecy never had its origin in the will of man, but men spoke from God as they were carried along by the Holy Spirit" (2 Peter 1:16, 20–21).

The fact the Bible said it was God's Word wasn't enough to convince me of its authorship and infallibility during my skeptical college days. "I could write a document and say it's God's Word, but that doesn't prove it is," I reasoned. "I could say I'm anyone or anything, but that wouldn't make it true." I also questioned whether men, whom I knew were imperfect, could transcribe a perfect document, especially when component books were separated by centuries. Ironically,

though, it was these factors—God's proclamation and man's im-
perfection—that convinced me the Bible is God's Word.

Fundamentally we believe by faith that God inspired the Bible. But
as we experience the Word and examine the evidence, the facts are difficult to ignore. There is no other book that can transform lives
supernaturally. Self-help books supply information, inspirational
books superficially touch our souls, but only God's Word has the spiritual power to deeply and irrevocably turn a person from wicked to
holy. Observing this capacity helped to convince me that God's
proclamation was true.

But what about those imperfect writers? God pulled off an aston-
ishing feat with them. He used more than forty different authors over
a period of fifteen hundred years and still wrote a book that is uncannily cohesive in its facts, message, and prophecies. Almost with a sense
of humor, God used a gallery of diverse and deficient men—priests,
kings, farmers, shepherds, physicians, tentmakers, fishermen, philoso-
phers—to create an accurate, unified work.[4] I decided I couldn't argue
with that.

I could cite other justifications for the Bible as God's Word, but
these particularly sparked my faith. Yet in spite of my questions,
despite anyone's doubts, the Bible is God's Word because He says it is.
He doesn't need our belief to make it so. He is Jehovah, the Self-
Existent One. Bible commentator Nathan Stone explains, "When we
read the name Jehovah, or LORD in capital letters in our Bible, we
think in terms of 'being' or existence and life, and we must think of
Jehovah as the Being who is absolutely self-existent, the One who in

Himself possesses essential life, permanent existence."[5] Only this One could create the everlasting Word and then perennially speak to humanity through it.

❦ *The Scriptures always endure.* Jesus said, "Heaven and earth will pass away, but my words will never pass away" (Mark 13:31). In 1947 shepherds stumbled across the first of the Dead Sea Scrolls in a Judean cave, giving the world biblical texts copied more than one thousand years ago—the oldest discovered manuscripts to date.[6] Despite wars and dissenters and lost civilizations, the Bible has endured spiritually in hearts but also physically through the hands of unknown copiers and passionate martyrs who ensured its survival and spread.

In the 1500s William Tyndale of England translated the Bible into English, despite the powerful pope's disfavor. Tyndale had heard a student say, "The Bible is not necessary. It is all foolishness to talk about translating it into English for the people to read. All they need is the word of the pope. We had better be without God's laws than the pope's laws!" Tyndale replied, "I will one day make the boy that drives the plow in England know more of the Scriptures than the pope does."

Soon English authorities spied on Tyndale, desiring to stop his translation, so he moved to Germany, the home of the first printing press. There Tyndale produced copies that he smuggled into his country in bales, barrels, and sacks. As authorities confiscated the Bibles, more crossed into England because the people hungered to read God's Word for themselves. Soon the Bible flourished in England, in a language the people understood, and from that country it spread to the world.

Lured back to England by spies and his own homesickness, Tyndale met up with authorities who hung him without a trial and burned his body immediately afterwards. Before the hanging he closed his eyes and prayed, "Lord, open the king of England's eyes."[7] Since then the Bible has been translated into more than two thousand languages. (In contrast, the works of William Shakespeare, the "master" of the English language, have been printed in fifty languages.) From the time its first word was scratched on a surface, the Bible has endured incredible odds to survive. It is still the best-selling book in the world.[8]

❦ *The Bible speaks the truth.* The psalmist sang, "because the word of the LORD is right and true; he is faithful in all he does" (Psalm 33:4). For those who think writers made up the biblical stories, the archaeological proofs of scriptural accuracy are becoming harder to ignore. Consider these examples: Skeptics debunked the existence of the Hittite empire, mentioned forty times in the Bible, until in 1906 archaeologists excavated its capital city and 100,000 clay tablets that documented the culture.[9] Historians denied the existence of King Arioch and King Sargon of the biblical books Genesis and Isaiah, respectively. Then in recent history archaeologists unearthed the foundation of their palaces and other artifacts. The Book of Joshua describes an occasion during war when the sun did not set for a day (10:13). For years this seemed mythical to experts, but now the three great record-keeping countries of the world—China, Egypt, and Greece—record 24 3/4 hours that can't be accounted for in time-keeping history: about a whole day.[10]

Increasingly, "unprovable" biblical facts and locations are being proved as the truth. But more important, God's Word is the moral truth—the compass by which He asks us to direct our actions. The Ten Commandments lay the foundation for God's morality, exposing our sin to God's perfection, yet the complete story about depravity and redemption, moral conduct and heaven's hope, permeates the entire Bible. We cannot separate the commandments from Christ's teachings or the apostles' admonitions, choosing which ones we prefer and tossing aside others. Because the Scriptures are God inspired, they constitute the whole truth about our relationship to Him and the world.

The Bible's truths are the underlying but unrecognized foundation for many countries' laws. But even without expressed laws, God's morality is stamped on the conscience, as if God said, "I'm putting My truth inside you, in case you don't read My Book." We can ignore the Bible and deny our consciences, but God's truth still resides within. Paul explained to the Roman church:

For God does not show favoritism.

All who sin apart from the law will also perish apart from the law, and all who sin under the law will be judged by the law. For it is not those who hear the law who are righteous in God's sight, but it is those who obey the law who will be declared righteous. *(Indeed, when Gentiles, who do not have the law, do by nature things required by the law, they are a law for themselves, even though they do not have the law, since they show that the requirements of the law are written on their*

hearts, their consciences also bearing witness, and their
thoughts now accusing, now even defending them.) This will
take place on the day when God will judge men's secrets
through Jesus Christ, as my gospel declares.

Romans 2:11–16, author's italics

❦ *God's Word doesn't change.* Jesus declared, "I tell you the
truth, until heaven and earth disappear, not the smallest letter, not the
least stroke of a pen, will by any means disappear from the Law until
everything is accomplished" (Matthew 5:18). Since the beginning of
time through each new moment today, God has not changed the message of His Word. He doesn't alter His morality for specific cultures
or overlook the transgressions of certain people. His commands not to
lie, steal, commit adultery, or worship other gods still apply today. So
if we want to hear God's voice through His Word, we can't twist the
words to fit our thinking or to rationalize sin.

Certainly, Christ redeemed us from the Old Testament laws, and
we live under grace, and there are cultural practices of biblical times we
don't follow today. But I'm referring again to God's morality—the
truth of the Scriptures—which has never changed. This last year I've
thought a lot about the unchangeableness of the Bible's directives. It's
been a time of grieving over friends' decisions to bend God's truth to
support their desires. Some have chosen engaging in casual sex, living
together as unmarried couples, practicing homosexuality, or following
a cult, either claiming Scripture irrelevant to contemporary lifestyles or
reinterpreting it to justify their actions. I've marveled at their ability to

ignore what the Bible clearly says about these sins, and I've dreaded the upcoming consequences. I love these friends dearly, and sin leads to pain.

True to His holy nature, though, God hasn't let me complain to Him about these friends. Instead, He's used my sadness to spotlight the areas in which I hedge Scripture or ignore what it says. He's been brokenhearted over my sins and partial obediences, asking that I adjust specific actions and attitudes to His Word. My acts of omission or quiet compromises may differ from these friends' transgressions, but nonetheless they are sins.

As a child I watched a television cartoon in which an elephant recited, "I said what I meant, and I meant what I said. An elephant's word is 100 percent." The Lord makes the same claim about His Word. Yesterday, today, and forever, He means what He has already said. To follow Him, we're to conform to Scripture instead of cleverly adjusting it to ourselves, remembering that God's Word is the path to joy and freedom. With the psalmist we can pray, "Direct me in the path of your commands, for there I find delight" (Psalm 119:35).

❦ *The Scriptures are reliable.* The Lord said to Jeremiah, "You have seen correctly, for I am watching to see that my word is fulfilled" (Jeremiah 1:12). With unbreakable tenacity, God sticks to His Word. He *means* what He says, and He *does* what He says, so what the Bible predicts or promises will eventually materialize. We can be assured that we'll reap what we sow, our sins will find us out, God restores the soul,

He forgives sin, the meek will inherit the earth, Jesus will come again, heaven and hell exist. Free will and Satan's tactics can muddle our faith, hindering Scripture's effect on us, but this doesn't render the Word any less reliable.

The Scriptures are also reliable in their ability to grant insight, wisdom, and solace. "Witness the man in the labour camp described by Solzhenitsyn, who had the bunk above his, and used to climb up into it in the evening, and take old, much-folded pieces of paper out of his pocket, and read them with evident satisfaction," wrote Malcolm Muggeridge, "It turned out that they had passages from the Gospels scribbled on them, which were his solace and joy in that terrible place. He would not, I feel sure, have been similarly comforted and edified by re-runs of old footage of religious TV programs."[1] Nothing compares to comfort from the God of the universe.

Like the Russian prisoner, we can find hope and help in the Bible each day. If we embrace the Word as inspired, enduring, truthful, unchangeable, and reliable, we will approach it with belief and reverence. "'Has not my hand made all these things, and so they came into being?' declares the LORD. 'This is the one I esteem: he who is humble and contrite in spirit, and trembles at my word'" (Isaiah 66:2). When we humbly respect God's Word, we can be assured that through its pages God will speak to us. We can stand on its promises without doubt and move forward with faith and confidence. In all facets of life, the Bible becomes our dependable companion.

Daily Words for Everyday Life

A new Christian turns to me and says, "You know, before I became a believer, the Bible didn't make sense to me. Now it's clear and speaks to me all the time. What happened?"

What "happened" was the Holy Spirit. Before His departure from earth, Jesus told the disciples, "But the Counselor, the Holy Spirit, whom the Father will send in my name, will teach you all things and will remind you of everything I have said to you" (John 14:26). At conversion the Holy Spirit invades us and enlightens our spiritual eyes. The Bible becomes a personally illuminated manuscript, artistically full of color and detail, yet amazingly readable and practical. And in the midst of life, the Spirit brings biblical truths to mind at just the right time to teach, rebuke, correct, and train us in righteousness (2 Timothy 3:16) or to speak to us about anything the Father wants to say.

Obviously, to hear God's voice in Scripture we need to spend time reading and pondering it. In his book *My Friend, the Bible,* John Sherrill described his personal quest to understand and apply the Scriptures to his daily life. As he spent more time in the Bible, he discovered two kinds of verses that infuse God's "mystic energy" into our souls and prepare us for life's challenges.

🦌 *Manna verses* speak to us daily. God quickens our spirits as we read these Scriptures, and often they immediately apply to day-to-day living. Sherrill said these verses "emphasize the elusive nature of our relationship with God. We need to come to Him daily for a new supply of Himself. We can't capture Him, box Him."

We gather up manna verses during devotional times or by merely reading Scripture. During these reading sessions, we don't need to jump from book to book, looking for a passage that's meaningful to us. We can simply "fill up" on God's Word, reading the next passage in a structured plan or soaking up Scripture as the Spirit prompts us. As we plod along, faithfully reading what comes next, God can speak to us. Sometimes the words speak generally to our overall lives, some-times specifically to that day.

"When I read through the Word or do a Bible study, just open-ing up to the next text, it's amazing how God speaks to me through a verse or passage," says my friend Kathy. "I mean, He speaks to me about something in my life that day! There it is, on the printed page, waiting for me."

Kathy has experienced the Bible's ability to speak to us personally through *rhema* verses, the word made personal to us. (*Rhema* is Greek for "living word.") When we receive a *rhema* message from the Lord through His written Word, it usually resonates deep within us. Often the words uncannily speak to a situation we're in and enlighten us with supernatural wisdom. They can be a solution to a current problem, a message of divine comfort, or words of warning or admonition.

But Kathy doesn't stop there. For each passage Kathy reads, she writes its key or main theme verse in a journal, along with cross refer-ences. Days or weeks later, as Kathy reviews her notes, she often notices a general theme emerging. Again, the theme addresses an issue, a rela-tionship, a special guidance, or something else relevant to her life. She meditates on these words, and manna verses begin turning into arsenal verses.

❧ *Arsenal verses* emphasize the opposite principle of manna verses. Through memorization, meditation, and recall, these verses store in our brains for a time when we need them. At the right moment they march through our thoughts to guide our actions.

"God's Word is also imperishable, inexhaustible, eternal," explained Sherrill, "and it can be stored up just as swords can be stored in an arsenal."[12] We also "store up" through extended study of biblical passages, books, words, and concepts.

When archaeologists discovered wheat seeds in the pyramids of 2500 B.C., placed there for the dead Pharaoh if he got hungry, they rejoiced. If they could analyze the ancient particles, it could help engineer new types of wheat for the future. Then when scientists planted the forty-five-hundred-year-old seeds, they grew and stirred more excitement. Seeds need three conditions for survival: darkness, dryness, and cool temperatures, and the pyramids had provided them all.[13]

The Bible compares its words to seeds, and if we store them in the right conditions of a tender and hearing heart, they will spring up in our lives, even if it's years later. (Actually, stored-up Scriptures also confront the hardened heart, but the soft and sifted soul is most fertile, allowing God's seed to take root and grow.) Many of the Bible verses I learned as a girl in Sunday school rise up to teach and convict me today at unexpected but opportune times. Sometimes I don't want to hear the message, but the words are persistent. They were sown by God.

Through the prophet Isaiah, the Lord proclaimed, "As the rain and the snow come down from heaven, and do not return to it without watering the earth and making it bud and flourish, so that it yields seed for the sower and bread for the eater, so is my word that goes out from my mouth: It will not return to me empty, but will accomplish what I desire and achieve the purpose for which I sent it" (Isaiah 55:10–11).

Personal Promises from God

Last night before nestling under a pile of blankets I pulled out a small hardback journal from a bookcase near my bed. Nearly twenty years ago when I expressed a desire to write books for Christians, I began jotting Bible verses into its pages. My dream looked impossible, but I felt God had given me scriptural promises for its fulfillment. I'd originally found these verses during devotional times, and though I'd read them before, they leapt off the page with new meaning, as if God had created the words just for me.

For a couple of years I added more verses, and a pattern emerged, though I still hadn't written much. God actually confirmed His calling to me in several ways, but here are examples of how He communicated it through Scripture:

❦ _About waiting for the promise to be fulfilled:_ "For God's gifts and His call are irrevocable. [He never withdraws them when once they are given, and He does not change His mind about those to whom He gives His grace or to whom He sends His call]" (Romans 11:29, AMP).

❦ _At the end of my first writers' conference (as a much-afraid student):_ "Go then, eat your bread in happiness, and drink your wine with a cheerful heart; for God has already approved your works" (Ecclesiastes 9:7, NASB).

 About the nature of my writing: "In addition to being a wise man, the Preacher [writer] also taught the people knowledge; and he pondered, searched out and arranged many proverbs. The Preacher [writer] sought to find delightful words and to write words of truth correctly" (Ecclesiastes 12:9–10, NASB, author's annotations).

Occasionally reviewing these verses fills me with wonder for God's faithfulness. He has fulfilled His promises to me: I've published over twenty books. But even more, I'm touched with new hope. If God has been this faithful in the past, He will be equally trustworthy in the future, especially with His still-unfulfilled promises.

It's not uncommon for God to give His children promises from the Scriptures, verses that glimpse into the future, give us hope, and encourage us to wait for their fulfillment. But as with all *rhema* verses, either daily manna or future promises, they can't be manufactured at will. God initiates this communication through the Holy Spirit, so as badly as we may need reassurances from the Lord, the open-the-Bible-and-point-to-a-verse method isn't advisable. In fact, it can be tremendously faulty.

Most of us know the story about the man who closed his eyes, pointed to a verse, peeked at the finger-marked place, and read, "So Judas...went away and hanged himself" (Matthew 27:5). Unhappy with that verse, he tried again and read, "Go and do likewise" (Luke 10:37). This story has been told so many times it's become a silly cliché, but we are just as careless if we embark on a similar method of guidance for the future. We can't force God to speak to us on our timetable, in a predetermined time and way. But if we consistently abide in His Word, He will speak in a gracious, unexpected, and individualized manner.

Granted, there are times when we open the Bible and a verse or passage pops out at us, handing up crucial insight. This verse could be a personal message from God, but wisdom doesn't run off in new directions based on one pop-up verse. It weighs the possible *rhema* verse(s) against the totality of God's communication with us.

"I'm embarrassed to tell you this," a friend writes to me from California. "I don't usually rely on this form of communication from God, but I opened my Bible, and my eyes landed on a verse that clinched my decision to attend school." Reading her admission, at first I was surprised. My rational- and deliberate-thinking friend making a decision by flipping open to a verse? It didn't sound like her. But as I read further, she explained the poignant ways God had been leading and confirming her decision to attend graduate school. The unexpected verse capped off a string of communication from God; its guidance didn't stand alone and almost felt like overkill. By the time she received the surprising *rhema* verse, she proverbially threw up her hands to say, "Ok, God, I get it! I get it! You've told me enough times. I'm going to school!"

If we're not sure if a message is from our Creator, often we can take a "time will tell" stance. This isn't an act of unbelief. It is a patient, expectant attitude that treasures the words in our hearts but wisely waits for God to bring them to life.

From the Obvious to the Obscure

Even when we consistently read the Bible, waiting for God to express His guidance, at times we need actively to seek His mind on specific topics.

🦌 *Stating the obvious.* Sometimes we run from book to book, person to person, and sermon to sermon seeking advice and reassurance when God has already stated His response to our dilemma in His Book. It may sound unspiritual, but in many instances we don't have to implore God because it'd be asking Him to state the obvious. We only need to recall or look up what the Bible says. God isn't going to give us a new enlightenment that contradicts His Word, and we'd save ourselves pain and frustration by obeying what He's already clearly stated.

Consequently, we can begin our search by examining what's in plain sight. Should I help a Christian in true financial need? Romans 12:13 says, "Share with God's people who are in need." First John 3:17 adds, "If anyone has material possessions and sees his brother in need but has no pity on him, how can the love of God be in him?" Do I start up a business partnership with a nonbeliever? Second Corinthians 6:14–15 advises, "Do not be yoked together with unbelievers. For what do righteousness and wickedness have in common? Or what fellowship can light have with darkness? What harmony is there between Christ and Belial? What does a believer have in common with an unbeliever?" Am I to forgive the person who offended me? Jesus said in Matthew 6:14–15, "For if you forgive men when they sin against you, your heavenly Father will also forgive you. But if you do not forgive men their sins, your Father will not forgive your sins."

Still, we can skirt the obvious—asking questions, looking for nuances and exceptions, reinterpreting the words—so we don't have to obey. (I count myself among the guilty.) The flesh is weak, and the tendency to complicate God's words is strong.

Most of us can relate to this fictional twist on the disciples' response to Christ's presentation of the beatitudes.

Then Jesus took His disciples up the mountain and gathering them around him, he taught them saying:

"Blessed are the poor in spirit for theirs is the Kingdom of heaven.

"Blessed are the meek.

"Blessed are they that mourn.

"Blessed are the merciful.

"Blessed are they who thirst for justice.

"Blessed are you when persecuted.

"Blessed are you when you suffer.

"Be glad and rejoice for your reward is great in heaven."

Then Simon Peter said, "Do we have to write this down?"

And Andrew said, "Are we supposed to know this?"

And James said, "Will we have a test on it?"

And Bartholomew said, "Do we have to hand this in?"

And John said the other disciples didn't have to learn this.

And Matthew said, "When do we get out of here?"

And Judas said, "What does this have to do with real life?"

Then one of the Pharisees present asked to see Jesus' lesson plans and inquired of Jesus His terminal objectives in the
cognitive domain.

And Jesus wept....[14]

🌱 *Digging for insight.* Is the answer not so obvious? Do we want
to learn all the Bible says about a word or topic? Would saturating our
souls with the Word help us release a sin or endure during difficult
days? Do we want to understand a verse, chapter, or book in context
to the whole Bible or the culture in which it was written? We can
proverbially roll up our sleeves and dig for biblical insight. Along with
Paul's protégé Timothy, we can "Study to shew [ourselves] approved
unto God, a workman that needeth not to be ashamed, rightly dividing the word of truth" (2 Timothy 2:15, KJV).

As we study, the emphasis should be on "rightly dividing" the
Word—understanding what God meant to say because some word
meanings have changed since biblical times. Respected Bible teacher
Evelyn Christenson suggests we observe what a passage says, interpret
it in relationship to its textual context, biblical culture, and original
languages, and apply it to our lives. Bible translations, a concordance, a
commentary, a Bible dictionary, Hebrew and Greek lexicons, or even
an atlas can assist in- depth study and even devotional reading.

But if we're listening for God's voice, beware of "dissecting the
Bible to death" and killing its ability to speak personally. Christenson
cautions that when we study, there must be a proper balance between
inspiration and perspiration. She recalls, "I used to bring home all the

reference books from my pastor husband's library for the study of next Sunday's lesson, stack them on the dining room table [the pile was usually at least two feet high], and systematically wade through them all week.... [But God] taught me there was a proper balance between what other people had to say and what He had to say. A seminary senior, in tears, confided to me, 'I've dissected the Scriptures so long that they don't say anything to me anymore.' My college botany professor gave us some profound advice: 'Remember, after you do enough dissecting, you no longer have a flower.'...But there is also the danger of all observation with little or no perspiration. By striking a happy medium and not neglecting either, God produced a good balance for me."[15]

Striking a balance between devotional reading and in-depth study also reminds us that what God says He asks us to obey. Jesus told the religious leaders of His day, "You diligently study the Scriptures because you think that by them you possess eternal life. These are the Scriptures that testify about me, yet you refuse to come to me to have life" (John 5:39–40). It's possible to religiously study the Bible but never apply the words to ourselves.

But what about topics that Scripture never addresses? Here we can ask, "Would the action lead to sin? Would it conflict with any principles stated in the Bible? Does it violate wisdom or the advice of godly people? Does it trouble the conscience?" If we answer no to each question, we guard against distress.

However we search the Scriptures for God's already spoken word, we haven't exhausted the ways He speaks to us. We can take the next step of listening for inner impressions of the soul.

Chapter Four

Listening to the Soul

*The Kingdom of God is founded on a personal knowledge
of the Lord which comes through a direct speaking
by him and a direct hearing by you and me.*

WATCHMAN NEE

"When are you going to bring this message to the Japanese?" a friend asks me after he hears one of my lectures. Until then I have worked only in America and Europe, Japan being far from my thoughts.

In my quiet time the instructions come distinctly: "Go to Japan."

I almost answer, "Yes, but..."

Obedience says, "Yes, Lord," and I have learned to obey.

I want to say, "Yes, but I know nobody there; I can't speak the language and it is so expensive." Again and again I begin counting and forget that my heavenly Treasurer reckons differently from me. The money comes, enough for a flight to Tokyo, where I arrive safely.

It is raining, and from the air Tokyo looks dark and dreary. I am not at all sure of myself. In the customs office a man asks me where he is to take my suitcase. I tell him I do not know.

"Is someone going to meet you?"

"No; nobody."

He feels sorry for me and offers to find me a hotel.

"Yes, if you please—and if possible one where English, German, or Dutch is spoken."

In his own car he takes me to a hotel. It is small, dirty, and dark, but the manager understands some English. But now there is a conflict in my soul. Was that really God's guidance? What if it was a mistake? I hardly dare to go out of doors for fear I might lose my way back to the hotel. Who would understand me? It becomes a real temptation from Satan. How terribly God's children are tempted in these times. It is as though Satan knows his time is running out. Then I read in 1 Peter 1 in Phillips' Letters to Young Churches about the glorious inheritance in heaven for me, and in the meantime we are guarded by God's power until we enter fully into that heritage—the only life insurance we can collect after our death.

"This means tremendous joy to you, I know, even though at present you are temporarily harassed by all kinds of trials and temptations," says the text. "This is no accident—it happens to prove your faith, which is infinitely more valuable than gold, and gold as you know, even though it is ultimately perishable, must be purified by fire. This proving of your faith is planned to bring you praise and honour and glory in the day when Jesus Christ reveals Himself."

No accident—planned! Not by accident, God's plan. But why?

To bring praise and glory on the great day of Christ's return. How glorious to catch a glimpse of that great plan and to see your own troubles as a tiny part of that plan. God makes no mistakes!

How it happens I cannot explain, but trust takes the place of doubt, and I can say, "Lord, I know I am safe in Your everlasting arms. You are guiding me and will surely make the next step plain."

Then comes to mind: "David Morken."

Is that God's answer? Years ago I met David at a Youth for Christ meeting, and he told me then that he might be sent to Japan. Fortunately, the telephone directory is printed in English, and there is his name, "David Morken, Director of Youth for Christ, Tokyo."

How wonderful, for the next step is clear. I pick up the telephone and hear a voice saying, "Mashie, mashie, mushie, mushie." In confusion I replace the receiver. I cannot even telephone in this strange land of strange people speaking a strange language. Finally, the manager gets the number for me, and I speak to David Morken.

"Hello. This is Corrie ten Boom speaking."

"What! Where are you?"

"Here in Tokyo."

"With whom?"

"Alone."

"But Corrie, how could you? You can't speak Japanese. If this isn't just like you, to come alone to a country where you can't understand the language!"

"It isn't my doing. I'm not enjoying this at all. It is God's doing, sending me here."

"OK. Always obey what God tells you to do. I'll help you. Go to the Central Railway Station, and I'll meet you with my car."

He did not offer to come to the hotel because it is hard to locate places in Tokyo. The first house built in a street is No. 1, the second, No. 2, even though it may be a half a mile farther down the street. Hence the numbers mean nothing.

"How do I find the station?"

"Take a taxi."

"What must I say to the taxi driver?"

"Ekki."

And true enough, I call a taxi driver and just say, "Ekki," and eventually arrive at the station, where David Morken awaits me. That day I am his guest, after which he secures a room for me in an Inter-Varsity Christian Fellowship house.

The first week I speak three times, the second week eighteen times, and the third week twenty-six times. A season of unusual blessing awaits me. How happy I am that I said, "Yes, Lord," instead of "Yes, but..."[1]

Slowly Growing in Grace

I must admit it. I'm not inclined to purchase a plane ticket to a foreign country without knowing the itinerary and accommodations ahead of time. Or to travel alone in a place where I can't speak the language. Even if I wanted to, friends and family would try talking me out of it.

"You just don't do things like that," they'd say. "It's foolish." But Corrie ten Boom did all that, and more. Corrie knew God's voice so well she played the fool for Him, and He blessed her faithfulness. In a shabby little hotel, alone and afraid, she recognized God's reassurance that with Him, nothing is an accident.

I admire such obedience. I'm also intimidated by it. My ability to hear God's voice pales next to hers. So when I'm prone to compare, I must remind myself that hearing His voice isn't a competition where the person who gets the most correct answers wins the game. I am to keep my eyes on God, tuning my ears to Him and learning His instruction for me. Hearing God's voice naturally flows out of a growing, spontaneous relationship with Him, not on keeping score. The focus is on knowing the loving Lord, not on how frequently I hear from Him and how accurately I assess what He just said.

This task can be difficult when people give testimonies at church or I'm with someone who continually says, "The Lord told me..." My tendency is to judge either myself or her. I might think, *Wow, I don't hear from God that way. What's wrong with me?* Or, *Is she right or just loony?* My need is to praise God with her or to quietly let time prove whether the person really heard from Him. Unless, of course, she is in spiritual danger or obviously on the wrong track. Then Scripture says I'm to warn her.

Above all, I'm not to boast about my ability to hear from God, as if I've attained a superior level of spirituality. I'm to boast in the Lord. The prophet Jeremiah said, "'Let not the wise man boast of his wisdom or the strong man boast of his strength or the rich man boast of his riches, but let him who boasts boast about this: that he understands and knows me, that I am the LORD, who exercises kindness, justice and righteousness on earth, for in these I delight,' declares the LORD" (9:23–24).

Still, it's honorable to desire hearing from God directly, without the props of people and programs. To hear His gentle voice within, in our quiet times and everyday moments, is a heart's delight. But be assured: Most of us don't begin at Corrie's level of sensitivity. At the time of this Japanese trip, Corrie was in her sixties. She'd learned to discern God's voice through years of hardship and obedience. And even the revered Corrie ten Boom, the remarkable concentration-camp survivor, made mistakes along the way.

As we grow in God's grace, we develop our ability to hear God one-on-one, through inner impressions on the soul. By trial and error, faithfulness and obedience, we recognize God's voice via thoughts that come to mind or inner compellings. But how do we develop this spiritual sensitivity? We begin by learning to recognize the sound of His voice.

The Sound of His Voice

What does God's voice sound like?

As a young Christian, I asked this question many times, and I seldom received a workable answer. In the Bible God's voice traveled a range of volumes and intensities, depending on the situation. He thundered when defending His people (Psalm 18:13). After a windstorm, earthquake, and fire, He whispered to Elijah at the mouth of an isolated cave (1 Kings 19:11–13). But what would be the nature of His voice if He spoke to me personally, in the recesses of my heart? I've had to answer that question myself, being willing to wait, listen, and more often than not, learn from my blunders.

In one sense, we all have to identify God's voice by ourselves. He speaks uniquely to each of us, and from experience we learn whether we're hearing God or our imagination or even the devil's deceptive voice. At the same time, it helps to learn how other believers discern His voice and what prompts them to act on what they've heard. So in the past few months I've conducted an experiment. When people have said, "God told me," I've asked, "How do you know He told you?" The answers have varied. Some people sputtered vague explanations and couldn't offer concrete descriptions. Others described specific signposts and feelings that identified God's voice to them. It's been an intriguing commentary on how blithely we can claim we've heard from God, when perhaps we're not really sure.

Collectively, though, from my experience and theirs, a two-pronged pattern seems common. Sometimes the Holy Spirit impresses a thought upon our minds; sometimes He stirs our hearts. If He speaks to the mind, it's usually a thought that intrudes upon the brain and is markedly different from what we've been thinking about. It possesses a distinct quality that causes us to say, "I wouldn't have considered that myself!" and suddenly gives us enlightenment into people or situations. If the Spirit speaks to the heart, it's often through a nudge that compels us to action, or a sense of restraint that warns us not to move forward. The mind and the heart can also sync, with a thought that agrees with an inner impression.

Lest this still sounds too ethereal, I'll share some personal examples.

After fifteen years of hardy service, my Escort finally needed to retire. I sold it for a pittance and purchased a new Kia Sportage, a sports utility vehicle. What a change! I'd grown so accustomed to driving an old "beater," I hadn't realized how smoothly and swiftly a vehicle could travel.

In the first month, however, the "swiftly" aspect got me into trouble. In a hurry to attend a meeting at my publisher's office, I picked up speed on a stretch near my home, and a policeman's radar clocked me at ten miles over the limit.

I'm not a speeder, I thought. *I get parking tickets, but I don't speed.* But the ticket and a seventy-five dollar fine disagreed with me. For the next two months I carefully monitored my speedometer, recognizing that the Sportage revved up much faster than the Escort did. (With the Escort, the difficulty was getting *up* to the speed limit.)

Then one day after a visit to the dentist, I decided to stop by the publisher's office again. As I drove toward that neighborhood, a voice inside said, *Go home.*

"That's a weird thought," I muttered to myself.

Go home, it said again, but I didn't listen and proceeded.

An hour later, after finishing up some minor business (which I really didn't need to stop by the office to do), I turned a corner and headed down the same infamous stretch toward my house. Within moments I heard the siren and spotted the flashing lights. It was the same policeman who'd caught me before, lurking on the same side street with his radar. Once again I was driving ten miles over the speed limit, but this time the ticket doubled to $150.

I felt both numb and irked. If I'd listened to that inner voice and gone home as instructed, I would have driven to my house from a different direction.

"Oh, Lord," I sighed. "What are you trying to teach me?" I expected an intensely spiritual answer like "absolute obedience" or "continual brokenness."

Instead, the words crossed my brain: *Slow down.*

At times God's messages flashed to the brain can be annoyingly pragmatic. Monitoring my driving since then (I can't afford to earn another ticket!), I've realized that yes, I do tend to speed. The vehicle wasn't to blame; I was, and I needed to change.

Another incident, still fresh in my mind after eighteen years, first taught me about God's warnings expressed as inner reservations. At the time a man moved into an apartment across the hall from me. He was amiable, spiritually inclined, and we often talked in the stairwell. "You ought to visit my church sometime," he told me.

"Ok," I said without thinking, but internally I felt as though an alarm had sounded. After that, each time we chatted I felt a jarring within, or what some people call a "check" in my spirit.

I never attended church with the man, and later I discovered that he belonged to a cult. When I found out, I immediately recognized that God had warned and most likely protected me from something spiritually harmful. I never uncovered exactly what the damaging element would have been, but I'm comforted to understand that God touched my soul with His hand of protection.

Some Guiding Characteristics

However God speaks to our souls—in our quiet times of reading and prayer, in the hum of a scheduled day—there are some guiding characteristics by which we can discern whether an inner message is from Him. Keep in mind, though, that we can't fit God into a formula and always predict how He will communicate with us. Consequently, these are guidelines based on a collection of people's wisdom, not etched-in-stone rules.

❦ *God speaks with clarity.* "His sheep follow him because they know his voice" (John 10:4). Over time we learn to recognize the quality of God's voice and how He sounds to us. We can be assured, though, that He doesn't speak in fuzzy generalities. If the message muddles, we probably need to wait until the communication clarifies. God's voice and messages are clear. Though we may need to wait for the Lord's confirmation, often when He speaks, we *know* He has spoken to us.

For example, my friend Joan has been seeking God about a direction for her life. Several months ago while driving to the airport, her car was hit from behind by another vehicle, and as she and a friend spun out of control, they yelled, "Jesus! Jesus, help us!" They could have been killed in that accident, but the car stopped and astonishingly, the two women weren't hurt. However, when Joan stepped out of the car, she said, "I'm supposed to be in the ministry." Though human error caused the accident, God used the circumstances to speak to her, and without question she knew it. The risk of losing her life made His voice very clear.

For a time, God may stir our hearts with a general sense that "something's up" and a change or direction is forthcoming. This holy restlessness causes us to seek God's will and prepares our hearts for His message, but when He finally speaks, it's with clarity. We transition from "I think God might be speaking to me" to "I know that He spoke to me."

❧ *God's voice is specific.* "Whether you turn to the right or to the left, your ears will hear a voice behind you, saying, 'This is the way; walk in it'" (Isaiah 30:21). The specificity of God's message relates closely to the clarity of His voice, and often the two characteristics are so intertwined they can't be separated. Like Corrie who first heard the words, "Go to Japan," we may receive only one-step-at-a-time direction, but the guidance is still specific.

Last year my sister called to say Mom needed a hundred dollars to help purchase new glasses. Could I contribute that amount?

"Yes," I said without considering my financial status. "I'll be glad to help." At the time I didn't have enough money to pay my own bills, but I believe that if I honor my mother and take care of her, God will provide for me. I felt God wanted me to mail the money to Mom, but in spite of this, I still asked the Lord, "How are you going to pull off this one?"

A few days later a friend stopped by my house and handed me a check for $100.

"I know it's rough financially, and I thought you could use this," she smiled, explaining that God had asked her to give me that amount.

The next day my friend left for a trip to visit her aging aunt in another state. Not long after she walked into her aunt's house, an uncle said to her, "I know it's expensive to travel, so here's $100 to defray your costs."

Neither my friend nor I expected to be rewarded for giving, and especially so precisely. Reviewing the chain of events I realized that in reality, an aging uncle from the East Coast paid for my mother's glasses! But isn't that like God? Specific, with dashes of surprise and humor tucked in.

❦ *God is not in a hurry.* "But do not forget this one thing, dear friends: With the Lord a day is like a thousand years, and a thousand years are like a day" (2 Peter 3:8).

An old bit of spiritual wisdom claims that God never runs, He walks. And like Enoch who "walked with God" (Genesis 5:22), He invites us to plod along with Him.

God also has been described as a "slow and certain light," so if we're in a hurry to do what we think He's telling us, we need to check our sources. God may quietly urge us along, but He doesn't create compulsiveness. This behavior emerges from fleshly desires or devilish influences. If we're intent on doing something "this minute, and I'm not willing to wait," unless it's a true emergency, the voice we're listening to probably isn't God's. A general rule of thumb is: God prompts, but the devil pushes.

On the other hand, there are times God asks us to operate quickly. But these are still acts of obedience, not obsessiveness. Many Christians tell stories of waiting on God for an extended time period, asking Him to move His hand or reveal His will. Then, from what seems like out of nowhere, God acts, and they scramble to rise up and follow. Note, however, that these incidences occur after a preamble of waiting the Lord.

I can think of several women who for years prayed and pleaded with God to bring them husbands. Then, when it seemed He'd turned a deaf ear to them, when they'd almost given up their last hope, the future spouse appeared unexpectedly, and the romance progressed quickly. For them, getting married meant waiting for God's timing.

❦ *God confirms His message.* "For I tell you that Christ has become a servant of the Jews on behalf of God's truth, to confirm the promises made to the patriarchs" (Romans 15:8). If the Lord is leading us toward action, He usually speaks through several mouthpieces. For example, we may hear His voice within. Then someone delivers an unmistakably similar message to us. In our Bible reading, *rhema* verses confirm what we've heard, and when we flip on the radio a preacher is using that same passage as His text! Finally, when we explain the concept to trusted advisers, they agree that the message sounds like God's voice. In other words, when He's guiding us, God usually doesn't speak in a vacuum. He confirms His words so we're certain of His directive.

If we're not sure whether God has spoken or precisely what He's saying, it's wise to wait for His confirmation. We can even ask Him to confirm His words to us through additional methods and messengers. My advice, however, is to wait for God's messages to flow toward us naturally, in the course of our days, rather than inventing a prefabricated sign as a measuring stick. A man once told me he challenged God, "If I'm to marry this woman, please have that streetlight turn off." Suddenly the light switched off, and he decided to propose.

I shuddered. If we test God with ridiculous requests, He may allow us to suffer the consequences.

❦ *God never contradicts His Word.* "The works of his hands are faithful and just; all his precepts are trustworthy. They are steadfast for ever and ever, done in faithfulness and uprightness" (Psalm 111:7—8). Whatever God speaks to us, He will never contradict the truth of His precepts found in the Bible. Friends have said to me, "I've perfect peace about this," when their course of action obviously violated God's Word. (To be fair, I confess I've done this myself.) Peace is not an indicator of the Lord's approval or guidance if the underlying motive or action contradicts Scripture and leads us into sin. When we're seek-ing guidance or making a decision, nothing can supersede the Bible's holiness and authority.

So the guideline is simple: If the message runs contrary to the Scriptures, it's not God's voice. He will confirm with His Word, but never will He contradict it.

The same is true if we speak on God's behalf. "It is no frivolous matter to hear the voice of God; and certainly it is an awesome thing to deign to speak for Him," muses Charles Colson in *Transforming Society.* "Luther said that preaching made his knees knock. Spurgeon, the brilliant British preacher, said he trembled lest he should misinter-pret the Word.

"So, the only way we can ever speak with confidence is to speak from the Word. Jesus gives us the best example: He knew the Scrip-tures, drew His authority from them, and based His words [and actions] upon them. Those who follow Him must do the same."[2]

❦ *God's voice corrects instead of accuses.* "Therefore, there is now no condemnation for those who are in Christ Jesus" (Romans 8:1). Though a later chapter addresses Satan's tactics and spiritual warfare, it's important to mention a related principle here. If we're walking with God, when the Holy Spirit speaks, He may reveal our sin, but He doesn't accuse us. If the voice we hear is accusatory, it belongs to the devil (Revelation 12:10). The accuser's voice shoves us toward depression and destruction.

"Are you allowing Satan to magnify the memories of your spiritual failures? He will always keep them before you unless you take your stand and move up in faith," explained the renowned minister A. W. Tozer.

"The devil will whisper, 'You didn't get very far along toward the deeper life, did you?'

"He will say, 'You made a big to-do about wanting to be filled with the Spirit and you really flopped, didn't you?'

"He will taunt you with the fact that you may have stumbled in the faith—and perhaps more than once! The devil wants you to live in a state of discouraged chagrin and remorse.

"Remember, the Bible does not teach that if a man falls down, he can never rise again. The fact that he falls is not the most important thing—but rather that he is forgiven and allows God to lift him up!"[3] Remember, too, that if God's voice does correct us, it is kind and cleansing, leading us to peace, healing, and joy.

❦ *God doesn't change His mind.* "I the LORD do not change" (Malachi 3:6). Ever meet someone who says she's sure of God's will for her but in a month she changes her mind? Then in a few more months she's certain it's something else? She probably hasn't heard from the Lord. When God calls us to a purpose or directs our steps, He does-n't career us down one path and then to another. He accompanies us on a steady journey, even though at the moment, the surrounding cir-cumstances don't make sense.

If we're running back and forth, we need to stop and wait on the Lord. The problem is, it's a human tendency to jump ahead of God, not being willing to wait until we're sure of His voice. And to be truthful, we can feel pressure from our spiritual community to be hear-ing from God. When people ask, "What is God saying to you about this situation?" it's hard to gulp and reply, I don't know. But be com-forted: When we're uncertain, it's not "unspiritual" to admit we're clueless about God's direction for now. Actually, we exhibit maturity by admitting we don't know and have decided to wait until we find out. God asks us to follow, not lead, and we can't follow until we're certain He's said, "Let's go."

All of these indicators of God's voice can be applied to the other ways we hear from Him: through the Scriptures, messengers, circum-stances, and the supernatural. But few if any of these factors will aid our discernment if we don't nurture a tender heart.

The Keeping of a Tender Heart

To discern God's inner impressions in the bustle of each day, we need to periodically hide away with Him, filling up on His presence and emptying out our sin, stress, and cluttered-up souls. Sitting at His feet, even if only for moments at a time, we learn to recognize His voice, and consequently it's easier to pinpoint the sound of His utterances amidst our routines, transitions, and emergencies. Most of all, time with God softens the heart, making it sensitive to His guidance.

"Give much time to quietness. For the most part we have to get our help directly from our God. We are here to help, not to be helped, and we must each learn to walk with God alone and feed on His Word so as to be nourished," advised the veteran missionary Amy Carmichael. "Don't only read and pray; listen. And don't evade the slightest whisper of guidance that comes. May God make you very sensitive, and very obedient."[4]

To keep a tender heart and open ears, we can follow the missionary's advice, represented in this poetic prayer by the Methodist minister John Wesley:

> Open, Lord, my inward ear;
> And bid my heart rejoice!
> Bid my quiet spirit hear
> Thy comfortable voice.
> Never in the whirlwind found,
> Or where the earthquakes rock the place;
> Still and silent is the sound,
> The whisper of Thy grace.
> From the world of sin, and noise,
> And hurry, I withdraw;

For the small and inward voice
I wait, with humble awe.
Silent am I now, and still,
Dare not in Thy presence move;
To my waiting soul reveal
The secret of Thy love.
Lord, my time is in Thine hand,
My soul to thee convert;
Thou canst make me understand,
Though I am slow of heart;
Thine, in whom I live and move,
Thine the work, the praise is Thine,
Thou art wisdom, power and love—
And all Thou art is mine.[5]

With this prayer on our lips, we ready ourselves to hear God's
voice, and to heed the call of His messengers.

Chapter Five

The Meaning of Messengers

Whether you are blessed with soul mates who settle
into the most comfortable room inside you,
or with those who walk with you just a little while,
not one of these people crosses your path by chance.
Each is a messenger, sent by God, to give you the wisdom,
companionship, comfort, or challenge you need
for a particular leg of your spiritual journey.

TRACI MULLINS

Near Rangoon, Burma, in the year *1795*, an encounter took place in the following manner:

"If the inhabitants of that village are not Burmese," asked a sun-helmeted English diplomat, "what do they call themselves?"

"Karen," replied the diplomat's Burmese guide.

"Carian," mispronounced the Englishman. The guide left the mistake uncorrected. A Scotsman could have duplicated the Asiatic way of flipping the tongue on an "r," but the guide had long ago given up trying to persuade Englishmen that the difference was worth mastering.

"Very well," said the Britisher. "Let's see what these 'Carianers' look like."

The "Carianers," it turned out, were even more interested to discover what the Englishman looked like! The first encounter with a European's white face electrified people in that village. Drawn like moths to a lamp, they converged upon the diplomat, who recoiled slightly as wiry brown hands reached out to touch his arms and cheeks.

The Burmese guide, meanwhile, spoke disparagingly of the Karen: "Be careful! They're just wild hill people given to stealing and fighting," he scoffed.

It was not entirely true. The Karen were in fact the most progressive of Burma's many tribal peoples. Burmese, however, had abused and exploited the Karen for centuries, making such descriptions self-fulfilling.

Nor could Burmese Buddhists forgive the Karen minority for stubbornly adhering to their own folk religion in the face of unremitting attempts by the Burmese to make Buddhists of them!

❧

The Englishman, in any case, was no longer listening to his guide. Cheerful Karen voices now charmed his ears. Every man, woman, and child around him flowed with radiant welcome. How refreshingly different, he thought, from the usual Burmese crowd's aloofness toward foreigners.

A Karen man who could speak Burmese explained something to the guide.

"This is most interesting," the guide said. "These tribesmen think you are a certain 'white brother' whom they as a people have been expecting from time immemorial!"

"How curious," replied the diplomat. "Ask them what this 'white brother' whom they as a people have been expecting is supposed to do when he arrives."

"He's supposed to bring them a book," the guide said. "A book just like one their forefathers lost long ago. They are asking—with bated breath—'hasn't he brought it?'"

"Ho! Ho!" the Englishman guffawed. "And who, pray tell, is the author whose book has power to charm illiterate folk like these?"

"They say the author is Y'wa—the Supreme God. They say also..." at this point the Burman's face began to darken with unease, "...that the white brother, having given them the lost book, will thereby set them free from all who oppress them."

The Burman began to fidget. The nerve of these Karen! The English diplomat was part of a team sent to arbitrate a dispute between Britain and Burma—a dispute which Burma feared might give Britain pretext to add Burma to its empire. And now these wily Karen were practically inviting the British to do just that! Who would have guessed, he fumed, that simple tribesmen could be capable of such subtlety?

Sensing the guide's displeasure, the Englishman also began to squirm. One word from the guide and Burmese authorities might descend with swords and spears against these humble villagers.

"Tell them they're mistaken," he ordered, hoping to set the Burman at ease. "I have no acquaintance with this god called Y'wa. Nor do I have the slightest idea who their 'white brother' could be."

Followed by the guide, the diplomat strode out of the village. Hundreds of Karen, palled with disappointment, watched them leave. They intended no political ploy. They had simply repeated in all sincerity a tradition which had haunted them as a people since antiquity.

"Could our forefathers have been mistaken?" asked a young Karen.

"Don't worry," responded an elder, managing a hopeful smile. "One day he will come. Other prophecies may fail, but not this one!"

❦

In 1871, a devout American Baptist missionary named Adoniram Judson disembarked near Rangoon, Burma, after a long sea journey from America. He had a Bible tucked under his arm, to be sure, but he possessed not the slightest inkling of the incredible significance that book held for more than three million people living within 800 miles of the dock on which he stood.

Judson found lodging in Rangoon. He learned the Burmese language with extreme care. At length, dressed in a yellow gown similar to those worn by Buddhist teachers in Burma, he ventured to Buddhist marketplaces and preached the gospel to Buddhist Burmese. Alas, Judson found little response. Often he struggled against an almost overpowering feeling of discouragement. Only after seven years of preaching did Judson find his first convert among the Buddhist Burmese!

All unknown to Judson, Karen people were passing daily by his home. Often they were singing, as their custom was, hymns to Y'wa— the true God. If only Judson could have learned their language too, he would have been startled by the content of those hymns! And he almost certainly would have found more response for the gospel among humble Karen people than his fondest dreams could anticipate. All unaware of the awesome potential of the Karen, an often disconsolate Judson turned increasingly to the task of translating the Bible into Burmese, since he had so few converts to occupy his time with counseling.

As it turned out, Judson's translation of the Bible into Burmese became foundational for all that his later-arriving colleagues were to accomplish among Burma's many minority peoples. If Judson himself had been caught up in a Karen-type response, he might never have found time to complete that translation!

☙

Then, as Providence arranged, a rawhide-tough Karen man came to the very household where Judson stayed. He was looking for work to help him pay a debt. Judson arranged employment for him. That man was Ko Thah-byu. He had a violent temper, and estimated that he had killed about 30 men during his former career as a robber!

Gradually Judson and other members of the household introduced Ko Thah-byu to the gospel of Jesus Christ. At first the Karen man's brain seemed too dense to grasp the message. Then a change took place. Ko Thah-byu began asking questions about the origin of the gospel and about these "white strangers" who had brought the message—and the book which contained it—from the west. Suddenly everything fell into place for Ko Thah-byu. His spirit received the love of Jesus Christ like dry land absorbing rain!

Around that time a newly recruited missionary couple—George and Sarah Boardman—arrived in Rangoon to assist Judson. George Boardman opened a school for illiterate converts. Ko Thah-byu had never dreamed of attending school. Now he quickly enrolled, for he was determined to learn to read that Burmese Bible as fast as Judson could translate it. To the amazement of Judson and Boardman, Ko Thah-byu manifested a total preoccupation with the Bible and its message.

For it had already dawned upon Ko Thah-byu that he was the very first among his people to learn that "the lost book" had actually surfaced in Burma! Accordingly, he also accepted his own responsibility to proclaim the good news that virtually every Karen was waiting to hear. So when George and Sarah Boardman announced plans to launch a new mission in the city of Tavoy, in the panhandle of southern Burma, Ko Thah-byu said eagerly, "I'll go with you."

They took him. As soon as they arrived in Tavoy, Ko Thah-byu begged Boardman to baptize him. Ko Thah-byu set out immediately on a journey into the hills of southern Burma. Each time he came to a Karen village, he preached the gospel. And almost every time he preached, virtually every Karen within earshot responded with wonder!

*Soon hundreds of Ko Thah-byu listeners came flocking to Tavoy to
see the "white brother" who had arrived at last with the book!*[11]

Looking for a Messenger

Looking for a messenger is as ancient as life itself. Since the Garden of
Eden, humanity has hungered for meaning, wanting the way to
redemption. Like the primitive Karen people, we've yearned for someone to tell us the truth, to point us to the One greater than ourselves.
In turn, God has answered our questions with Himself. Through
prophets, poets, kings, and priests, He has spoken to us. Even the
beloved Son served as a messenger, only speaking what the Father told
Him to say (John 8:28). The message was so sacred not even the Christ
would add to or subtract from it.

Undoubtedly, salvation is God's most important message to us,
but once we accept His forgiveness and new life, the messengers don't
stop crossing our path. Along with His Word and inner impressions
of the soul, God speaks to us through human mouths to help us grow
in grace. The combinations of who God selects and how He uses them
are virtually endless.

It may surprise us, but to get our attention He now and then
communicates through nonbelievers. They might deliver a compli-
ment, an off-handed remark, or an incisive barb that hands us
God-inspired truth and insight. But frequently it's our local Christian brothers and sisters who intentionally, and sometimes
unintentionally, voice God's encouragement, correction, and guidance

to us. The traveling evangelists and television preachers serve as conduits for God's messages, but most of hearing His voice occurs in up-close, ongoing relationships and community. This is what God intends for us.

"The first thing God did after He made man was to create someone who would be his counterpart—Eve, different from himself and yet his counterpart—so that there would be a proper, horizontal, finite, personal relationship as well as the vertical personal relationship with the infinite-personal Creator," explained the theologian Francis Schaeffer, who often wrote about Christian community. "That is what God wants. God has called us in the New Testament—in the Old as well, but in a slightly different form—to come into an understanding that there is to be community, a relationship between those who are already Christians." We form Christian community through marriage, family, friendships, church, small groups, organizations, and other groups that facilitate face-to-face and life-to-life encounters. We develop community to turn our spiritual words into practical realities, and this requires commitment.

When we join God's family, He calls us to the joys and tribulations of involvement. In true community we give and take love, hope, guidance, inspiration, and encouragement, but we also bump into one another's doubts and disappointments, faults and frustrations, troubles and trepidations. Scripture says, "As iron sharpens iron, so one man sharpens another" (Proverbs 27:17), but in the process, sparks can fly. Hopefully, we speak encouraging words to one another, but we are human, and we also say things that hurt. Not by accident, then, the

Bible also emphasizes our need to forgive. If we travel full circle—
speaking God's truth, making mistakes, and forgiving one
another—we grow in grace, love, intimacy, security, and acceptance.
And deep in our hearts, aren't these the gifts we want to receive?

I admit, though, that this process makes me nervous. I am a Baby
Boomer, cut from an artist's cloth, with a desire for independence. I
grew up in a church clutched by critical members, and I learned early
that believers can deliver wounding messages. Add to that years of
working in parachurch organizations, and I understand the wonders
and woes of spiritual community. Christians have poured love into me;
they also have inflicted pain. But they are not all to blame. I've also
pinpointed my ability to hurt people without knowing it. So in the
past few years, aside from relationships with friends, I've treaded lightly
in Christian community, recovering from the stress of troublesome
commitments.

Last year I began attending a new church, and for the first six
months I slipped in and out as an unidentified worshiper. I've wondered, *If I draw too close, what will these people say to me? Or worse
yet, what might I say to them?* The Lord, however, has other plans for
me. God has given me time to recover, but He's still underscoring that
as His followers we're to assemble together, encourage others toward
good works, rejoice and weep as a family, and bear one another's bur-
dens. In effect, we are to be God's messengers to one another, depositing
His hope and truth into hearts. I crave these relational bonds, but to
create them, I need to accept their inherent human imperfections,
including my own. I can't separate the delight from the difficulty.

However, when I think clearly about the facets of community, I admit that God's messengers to me have delivered many positive and encouraging words, which far outweigh the critical comments I've heard. They've echoed the Father's approval, compassion, and creativity. This, too, is what God intends. He intends this for us all. He sent angels with "good news of great joy" to *all people,* until the cessation of time (Luke 2:10, author's italics). "Listen up," He says to us. "I have good words for you."

Heralds of Glad Tidings

"How beautiful on the mountains are the feet of those who bring good news, who proclaim peace, who bring good tidings, who proclaim salvation, who say to Zion, 'Your God reigns!'" (Isaiah 52:7). God's messengers, be they soulmates or passersby, can be heralds of hope as we walk onward and upward. But we need to train our spiritual eyes to recognize their arrival and our ears to listen carefully. Contemporary messengers seldom look or sound like the prophets of old. They are our close friends on the phone, family members at the kitchen table, people we sit next to in church, the neighbors who bring over brownies. A casual conversation, observation, or other informal and unexpected means can unlock the insight we need.

In addition to these surprises, God also communicates through the spiritual gifts He distributes among His children. He bestows these gifts when we're filled with the Holy Spirit, and we all don't receive the same ones. God desires that we share our gifts with one another, creating an interrelatedness that meets our needs for companionship and spiritual enrichment. But most of all, spiritual gifts lead us toward maturity in Christ. "Each one should use whatever gift he has received to serve others, faithfully administering God's grace in its various forms...so that in all things God may be praised through Jesus Christ," explained the apostle Peter (1 Peter 4:10–11).

All gifts are important for a spiritual community's health, but not all fulfill an up-front role in a gathering or church service. Not all Christians agree about which gifts legitimately operate today, but we do concur that God grants many kinds of gifts to believers.[2] The Bible lists these gifts as: administration, apostleship, discerning of spirits (discrimination in spiritual matters), exhortation (encouragement), evangelism, faith, giving, healing, helps (assisting others), interpretation of tongues, knowledge (special understanding), leadership, mercy, miracles, shepherding (being a pastor), prophecy (inspired utterance, preaching), service (ministry), teaching, tongues (speaking in a never-learned language), wisdom.[3] Other gifts not specifically mentioned but notably functioning in the Body of Christ can be added to this list. For example, the gifts of hospitality and intercession.

Many of these gifts enable our spiritual brothers and sisters to serve as God's mouthpiece to us. An exhortation can provide the encouragement to persevere. A financial gift represents God's provision. Acts of mercy can express His forgiveness. A teacher or preacher can present a lesson or sermon that meets a specific need. Words of wisdom can put together the pieces of a puzzling situation. I've especially appreciated the comfort and guidance of messages delivered through spiritual gifts when I'm at a crossroads, wondering about the future.

Years ago, before becoming a writer, I joined a church in my hometown. During a special installation service the pastor prayed for each new member. As the minister prayed for me, he said, "God will fulfill your desire in writing and literature, and you will write into the night."

My internal response was, *What?*

The pastor had no idea that as a child I'd fantasized about being a writer. When he said these words, I'd given up on the dream but was wondering about my career path. Struck by my pastor's insight, I wrote his words in a journal. *We'll just see,* I thought, feeling mostly skeptical but also slightly hopeful. Not long after, God began impressing on me a call to write. In the next few years other people gave input similar to the pastor's, and my faith in God's calling grew.

Looking back, I marvel at how specific God's words were through His messenger. Some of my best writing time has been after ten o'clock at night. Through the years I'd forgotten this aspect of the prayer, and my late-night writing developed according to my schedule and natural body clock. Today, as I review my old journal and recognize that even this detail came true, I'm even more certain the pastor spoke God's good news to me.

A few years later, after moving away to work in Christian publishing, I visited that church while home on vacation. After the service I walked to the altar, and this pastor prayed for me again, not knowing the details of my life. Halfway through his prayer he stopped and asked, "Did you recently get passed over for a promotion at work?"

I lifted my bowed head and said, "Yes."

"God wants you to know that act was from Him," explained the pastor. "He has lessons for you to learn in this."

I was flabbergasted. Recently I'd been overlooked for a job title change from associate editor to editor—a promotion I felt was long overdue. I hadn't told anyone at home yet, so I knew these words had to be from God. But I was also angry. *Why would God do this to me?* Again, with hindsight I mark this incident as the beginning of God's unraveling the pride I had in positions and power. Today I don't think about titles, except when I'm asked to fill out author questionnaires, and I'm relieved. I'm not trying to prove my worth by how important my position sounds. (When I make new acquaintances, I don't even tell them what I do until they yank it out of me!) In this case, God's messenger brought words difficult for me to hear, but eventually I realized that His correction was in my best interest. It helped to loose me from bondage.

From this perspective, even God's messengers of correction bring us good news. Though they may inflict temporary pain with a warning or the raw truth, they may be pointing the way to freedom.

Don't Shoot the Messenger

"You know, your competitive attitude has caused problems with some of your friends," she ventured while sitting at my dining room table, watching me iron clothes in the kitchen.

"What?" I shot back. "Who told you that? You don't even live in this town! You're never around me long enough to know what I'm like." I wanted to throw the iron at her. Hurt and furious, I closed down the conversation as quickly as possible. She planned to stay the weekend, and I didn't want to spend it fighting. So I composed myself and played the gracious hostess, even though I felt horrible.

At that stage of my life, confrontation didn't seem like the "nice" thing to do, especially to a friend. So when this woman confronted me, I interpreted it as disloyalty and rejection. However, in the next few years her comment prompted me to evaluate my attitudes and uncovered a need for change. The discovery felt painful, but as I've opened myself up to God's spiritual rehabilitation, it's reaped precious rewards in relationships. I'm much less prone to compare and compete, which has de-stressed and relaxed me. Slowly I'm learning that if I don't shoot the messenger, she might prove valuable.

"I well believe, to unwilling ears; None love the messenger who brings bad news," wrote Sophocles in his play *Antigone*.4 Middle management will confirm how difficult the role of a go-between can be. Or police officers who deliver death announcements to unsuspecting families. Or even the well-meaning friend who wants to iron out kinks in a relationship. Most people don't like to bear bad news, but to use another cliché, in the spiritual realm somebody's got to do it. God has always employed middle men and women to tell people how they need to change and the possible consequences if they don't. Noah's ark warned of a coming flood. Moses blasted the Israelites for their golden calf. Esther saved a nation by approaching the king. Jeremiah begged God's people to repent. Jesus walked the earth for three years, preaching about eternal judgment. In these and other biblical incidents, a messenger risked life itself to deliver dire news—and the receivers' response determined their fate and relationship with God.

Hopefully, people who deliver negative or uncomfortable messages to us won't suffer as much as those in the Old and New Testaments. But if they are God's messengers, the risk in our response looms just as great. We can gratefully receive the truth about ourselves—or suffer the consequences of sin and woundedness. However, receiving negative input with graciousness isn't an easily acquired art form. It hurts when people point out our wounds, even when they speak tenderly and carefully. They've stuck their fingers in a bloody, internal injury, and we instinctively pull away. If we can't retreat, then we balk, disagree, fight back—anything to avoid facing our sins and flaws, or exposing our actions that hurt others, or discovering we're not on God's path.

However, when God sends a message, He insists on getting through. If we refuse one messenger, He sends another. In the interim we've probably persisted in the problem attitude or behavior, digging ourselves in deeper and tainting more relationships or barreling farther down a wrong road. To get our attention and extricate us from the wreckage, God uses His strong arm of love to discipline us. We ask, "Why is God being so hard on me?" when for a long time He's spoken to us quietly. Our inattention made Him pull out the megaphone.

We can choose, then, to receive God's messengers the "easy," less painful way instead of the hard, disciplinary way. We can listen and discern whether the message is from God and, if it is, take appropriate action. As we mature spiritually, we may even welcome these holy messengers. We realize that if we cooperate, God's words will heal, release bondages, and create peaceableness. Even His messages of correction are missives of love.

But what if a messenger isn't from God? Or someone delivers a needed message in a destructive way? What then?

The Pain of Messy Messengers

Forty-year-old Maggie recalls sitting on her front porch as a five-year-old child and feeling sad for no apparent reason. "It seems as though I've always been undermined by sadness," she says. In fact, she remembers every major part of her life more by its accompanying depression than its significant events.

"I tried everything—exercise, talk therapy, nutritional changes, prayer for inner healing and deliverance—to relieve the depression. But nothing worked," she explains. "I felt like a personal and spiritual failure."

The depression worsened with age and stress, and it began affecting Maggie's relationships at work. Some days she'd be open and nurturing. Other days, tense and demanding. "Ironically, I didn't know I was behaving this way," she says. "The depression was so much a part of me I couldn't see the forest because of the fog in the trees." But people at work could see, and the gossip about Maggie's moodiness ignited, damaging her reputation as a manager.

Then within a crushing forty-eight hours, an employee confronted Maggie, describing her distaste for the depressed woman. After this, she reported the same to Maggie's boss. Next, without getting Maggie's side of the story, he demoted and humiliated the struggling manager in front of her employees. Maggie's years of intense work on an important project poured down the drain, and with nowhere to turn, she thought about suicide.

"I think if one person had approached me with a bit of compassion and understanding, I would have recognized what I was doing But the woman who set off the devastating chain of events, though she insisted she was doing the 'Christian' thing, wounded me and the entire department," recalls Maggie. "If she'd chosen not to gossip and had presented her observations maturely, there wouldn't have been so much damage."

Maggie admits, however, that the woman's message held a kernel of truth. "The whole, horrible episode led me to get medical help for depression. I learned that my problem was genetic, handed down through my family, and that rolled some guilt off me. Within a few months, and ever since then, I've been free from the cloud over my head," she claims, her voice filled with relief. "I think God used a bad situation to point me toward healing."

Unfortunately, not all messengers possess good motives and utter loving words, and some message couriers are thoroughly evil, sent from Satan himself. But even those with good intentions can bungle the delivery, hurting instead of helping. Messy messengers arrive with an array of motivations, intentions, and styles, and instead of collapsing under their load of words, we need to practice discernment. After the initial frustration passes, we can ask, "Is there a kernel of truth in the message—something I need to listen to, even though the messenger was insensitive? Or is the messenger projecting his issues on me in the guise of spiritual concern? Or are both of these dynamics happening at once?"

"Deciding what was her problem and what was my problem was tricky," continues Maggie. "I knew this woman was in deep denial about herself, and I'd observed a number of weaknesses I wanted to throw back at her. Why is it that people with noticeable flaws wind up criticizing other people? Anyway, I didn't get a chance to retaliate, and with hindsight, I'm glad I didn't. I don't think God would have honored that. I needed Him to help me out of my own mire, so I concentrated on that. I prayed a lot, asking God to show me what was my responsibility to change and later worked on forgiving the woman who hurt me."

She pauses, then adds, "Forgiveness didn't happen overnight. It's been a process. Each time her name came to mind, I'd tell God, 'I forgive her.' She resigned from the job and left me and the mess behind her, and I realized that my anger and resentment would only hurt me. I think this helped me heal faster, and with time the pain faded."

Though there is no surefire formula for dealing with messy messengers, Maggie hit on several helpful actions if we're to find God's voice in the muddle. After we settle our initial emotions, inquiring prayer and an open heart are essential to the sorting-out process. So is forgiveness. With these in hand, we can uncover any kernels of truth.

Finding Kernels of Truth

Whether someone's words are encouraging or disruptive, neither type of message guarantees it's communication from the Lord. Unless it's something that resonates with us deeply and must be done immediately, we can step back and test the message for how it lines up with other communication we've received from God. Keeping in mind the characteristics of God, these guidelines can help.

❧ *Listen carefully.* Listen for what the person is actually saying, not for what you want to hear. Try not to color the message with prejudices, past pain, or personal issues. Don't interrupt. Concentrate on what's being said.

❧ *Respond thoughtfully.* It's easy to thank someone with a positive message, but also try to respond graciously to a person with criticism. Tell the person you'll consider the input, and try not to merely react by throwing back negative words.

❧ *Consider the message.* Does the message "witness" within your spirit? Does it uncannily fit your circumstances? After you've peeled away layers of pain or denial or confusion, is there a kernel of truth in the message? If the answer to any of these questions is yes, God may be speaking.

❧ *Consider the source.* Is this message from someone you trust? Is it delivered in a spirit of love and concern? When you set aside a messy messenger, does the message still ring true? Again, a yes answer to any of these could point to God's voice. Remember that no messenger is perfect and that people with their own, unresolved personal issues can still speak God's truth to you.

❦ *Check your attitude.* Is pride or disobedience making you resist the message? Perhaps pain or confusion? You may need to confess and deal with your barriers before discerning a message's validity.

❦ *Check for confirmation.* Look for confirmation through the other ways that God speaks, such as prayer, impressions of the soul, the truth of Scripture, other messages, spiritual gifts, the extraordinary.

❦ *Watch God move.* Often when we receive words from messengers, they explain what God is going to do. We don't have to run off immediately to make it happen. We can savor the message in our hearts and watch God fulfill His words to us. If the messenger describes something we need to alter, God will enable us to make the change.

These are only guidelines, not meant to quench the Holy Spirit but to keep us both wise and winsome as we interact with messengers. These qualities also benefit us if God calls us to be a messenger to someone else.

About Being a Messenger

Last week a friend of mine prepared for an anxiety-provoking surgery after an already difficult year. I told her I'd pray, and I asked God for angels to protect her. I don't consider myself gifted in intercession, but as I prayed for this friend, an image appeared in my mind's eye that filled me with comfort. Could God be giving me a reassuring message for my friend? The image was just as strong the next morning, the day of her surgery, so I sent my friend an e-mail message.

It read: "You have been on my heart a lot, and I have been praying for you. I have been praying for angels to guard and protect you today. As I prayed about this, I envisioned four guardian angels with you during the operation, each at a corner of the table you'll be lying on. As you look forward at the doctor, there will be an angel positioned at the left corner, holding a gleaming sword for your protection. At the right corner, there will be one of God's messengers with a vase of oil, for your healing. Behind you, by your left shoulder, an angel holds a cascading garland of flowers for your comfort. At your right shoulder, an angel holds a beautiful box. Out of it flows a sweet-smelling incense that ushers up to God. It is the wonderful aroma of people's prayers for you. As you prepare this morning, as the doctor works on you, as you recover, think of these guardians. But think, most of all, that God is with you."

My friend cried when she read the message and drew strength from these images while in the operating room. As I watched the clock tick slowly during her surgery, the angel descriptions reassured me too.

I love being this kind of messenger. Delivering hopeful words uplifts and satisfies both the recipient and the speaker. Our faith grows. It's giving corrective messages that unravels me. I'm aware of my own faults, and I don't like confrontation and rejection. Also, in the past I've delivered some messages insensitively, so I stall in this area, often missing important opportunities to speak up. It's taken years to learn that a well-timed corrective message, inspired by the Holy Spirit and delivered lovingly, also offers hope.

After watching a friend's behavior for a year, a few weeks ago I couldn't hold back any longer. I felt that emotionally and spiritually she was in danger. After reiterating my love for her, I pointed out the perilous behavior and what she could biblically do about it. She responded, "Thank you for speaking up. I've been looking for answers, wanting someone to tell me what to do." I admire her openness to input, and her response modeled how a hearing heart responds well to correction. I saw her last night, and already she's made changes and feels better, tuning her ears to God.

I don't profess expertise on being a messenger, but I've suggestions about message giving born from my own good and bad experiences.

🦌 *Discern if the message is from God.* We can give a message based on good intentions but still be inaccurate in what we say. For example, more than twenty years ago someone said to me, "God told me you're going to be married soon." I'm still single. These words and their outcome didn't hurt me, but it's best to ask God to confirm the message before we deliver it.

🦌 *Check the motivation.* In most cases messages are to be delivered for positive reasons—to help, heal, educate, encourage, admonish—rather than to spill anger, criticism, frustration, or exert control. Sometimes if we have unresolved issues, such as anger, we can sound angry when we speak. Express love, but at the same time, don't try to be a fix-it person. We are only couriers. It is God's job to institute change and fulfill His word.

🦌 *Wait for the right time.* Especially if we're giving a corrective message, the process can bungle because we don't temper ourselves to wait. Instead of discerning God's message and His timing, we rush into a situation, say whatever comes to mind, and leave behind debris.

Sometimes we may have an accurate message, but we've pre-empted the right time to deliver it.

❧ *Use God's name sparingly.* "God told me this about you" and "Thus saith the Lord" are powerful phrases. We can use them to offer hope or to sound important and authoritative. Sometimes we use these "God words" to heap guilt on someone and later confuse him or her if our words don't prove true. Even if we're sure a message is from God, it's not essential to say, "God told me." Message giving is an act of humility. God receives the credit, not us.

There are times, too, when God drops insight into our hearts but the best course of action is to say nothing at all. We are to pray for the individual or situation, expectant of the Miracle Maker's work on that person's behalf. Some of the most influential people in my life have been those who've quietly prayed for me until I've changed. After I've weathered the consequences of my stubborn will and finally submitted to God, they haven't said, "I told you so." With open arms, they've affirmed my progress.

Above all, message giving and receiving can be a celebration. We can revel in a God who cares to send messengers to meet our needs, clarify His will, and encourage us. Charles Dickens wrote, "Every human creature is constituted to be [a] profound secret and mystery to every other."[5] With the Spirit within and the joy of committed relationships, we can unravel the hidden places within, and pour in the mysteries of God. In turn, the mysteries will prepare us for the times when heaven comes calling through extraordinary doorways.

When Heaven Comes Calling

*In other world religions, miracles and legends
may be nonexistent or nonessential to faith.
Not so with Christianity.
Christ's birth was as miraculous as was his resurrection.
If we try to take away Christianity's miraculous heart, we destroy it.*

CALVIN MILLER

I saw a stranger at the front door and arose to meet him. He was tall and commanding in form, with a face of ineffable sweetness and beauty. Where had I seen him before? Sure, surely I had met him since I came [to heaven].

"Ah, I know!" I thought, "It is St. John, the beloved disciple." He had been pointed out to me one morning by the riverside.

"Peace be unto this house," was his salutation as he entered.

How his voice stirred and thrilled me! No wonder the Master loved him, with that voice and that face!

"Enter. Thou art a welcome guest. Enter, and I will call the mistress," I said, as I approached to bid him welcome.

"Nay, call her not. She knows that I am here; she will return," he said. "Sit thou awhile beside me," he continued, as he saw that I still stood, after I had seen him seated. He arose and led me to a seat near him, and like a child I did as I was bidden; still watching, always watching, the wonderful face before me.

"You have but lately come?" he said.

"Yes, I am here but a short time. So short that I know not how to reckon time as you count it here," I answered.

"Ah, that matters little," he said with a gentle smile. "Many cling always to the old reckoning and the earth-language. It is a link between the two lives; we would not have it otherwise. How does the change impress you? How do you find life here?"

"Ah," I said, "if they could only know! I never fully understood till now the meaning of that sublime passage, 'Eye hath not seen, nor ear heard, neither have entered into the heart of man, the things which God hath prepared for them that love him.' It is indeed past human conception." I spoke with deep feeling.

"'For them that love him'? Do you believe that all Christians truly love him?" he asked. "Do you think they love the Father for the gift of the Son and the Son because of the Father's love and mercy? Or is their worship oftentimes that of duty rather than love?" He spoke reflectively and gently.

"Oh," I said, "you who so well know the beloved Master—who were so loved by him—how can you doubt the love he must have inspired in all hearts who seek to know him?"

A radiant glow overspread the wonderful face, which he lifted, looking directly at me—the mist rolled away from before my eyes—and I
knew him! With a low cry of joy and adoration, I threw myself at his
feet, bathing them with happy tears. He gently stroked my bowed head
for a moment, then rising, lifted me to his side.

"My Savior—my King!" I whispered, clinging closely to him.

"Yes, and Elder Brother and Friend," he added, wiping away tenderly the tears stealing from beneath my closed eyelids.

"Yes, yes, 'the chiefest among ten thousand, and the One alto-
gether lovely!'" again I whispered.

"Ah, now you begin to meet the conditions of the new life! Like
many another, the changing of faith to sight with you has engendered
a little shrinking, a little fear. That is all wrong. Have you forgotten the
promise, 'I go to prepare a place for you; that where I am, there ye may
be also'? If you loved me when you could not see me except by faith,
love me more now when we have really become 'co-heirs of the
Father.' Come to me with all that perplexes or gladdens; come to the
Elder Brother always waiting to receive you with joy."

<hr />

Then he drew me to a seat, and conversed with me long and
earnestly, unfolding many of the mysteries of the divine life. I hung
upon his words; I drank in every tone of his voice; I watched eagerly
every line of the beloved face; and I was exalted, uplifted, upborne,
beyond the power of words to express. At length with a divine smile,
he arose.

"We will often meet," he said; and I, bending over, pressed my lips reverently to the hand still clasping my own. Then laying his hands a moment in blessing upon my bowed head, he passed noiselessly and swiftly from the house.

Then I turned and passed softly through the house to the beautiful entrance at the rear. Just before I reached the door I met my friend Mrs. Wickham. Before I could speak, she said: "I know all about it. Do not try to speak; I know your heart is full. I will see you very soon—there, go!" and she pushed me gently to the door.

❦

How my heart blessed her—for it indeed seemed sacrilege to try to talk on ordinary topics after this blessed experience. I did not follow the walk, but kept across the flowery turf, beneath the trees, till I reached home. I found my brother sitting upon the veranda, and as I ascended the steps he rose to meet me. When he looked into my face, he took both hands into his for an instant, and simply said, very gently: "Ah, I see. You have been with the Master!" and stepped aside almost reverently for me to enter the house.

I hastened to my room, and, dropping the draperies behind me at the door, I threw myself upon the couch, and with closed eyes lived over every instant I had spent in the hallowed Presence. I recalled every word and tone of the Savior's voice, and fastened the instructions he had given me indelibly upon my memory. I seemed to have been lifted to a higher plane of existence, to have drunk deeper draughts from the fountain of all good, since I had met "him who my soul loved."

It was a long, blessed communion that I held thus with my own soul on that hallowed day. When I looked upon the pictured face above me, I wondered that I had not at once recognized the Christ, the likeness was so perfect. But I concluded that for some wise purpose my "eyes were holden" until it was his pleasure that I should see him as he is.

When at last I arose, the soft golden twilight was about me, and I knelt by my couch, to offer my first praise in heaven. Up to this time in my life there had been a constant thanksgiving—there had seemed no room for petition. Now as I knelt all I could utter over and over, was: "I thank Thee, blessed Father; I thank Thee, I thank Thee!"

When I at last descended the stairs, I found my brother...and, going to him, I said softly: "Frank, what do you do in heaven when you want to pray?"

"We praise!" he answered.

"Then let us praise now," I said.

And standing there, with clasped hands, we lifted up our hearts and voices in a hymn of praise to God; my brother with his clear, strong voice leading, I following. As the first notes sounded, I thought the roof echoed them; but I soon found that other voices blended with ours, until the whole house seemed filled with unseen singers. Such a grand hymn of praise earth never heard. And as the hymn went on, I recognized many dear voices from the past—Will Griggs' pathetic tenor, Mary Allis's exquisite soprano, and many another voice that wakened memories of the long ago. Then as I heard sweet child voices, and looked up, I saw above us such a cloud of radiant baby faces as flooded my heart with joy. The room seemed filled with them.

"Oh, what a life—what a divine life!" I whispered, as, after standing until the last lingering notes had died away, my brother and I returned to the veranda....

"You are only in the first pages of its record," he said. "Oh, its blessedness must be gradually unfolded to us, or we could not, even here, bear its dazzling glory."

Then followed an hour of hallowed intercourse, when he led my soul still deeper into the mysteries of the glorious life upon which I had now entered. He taught me; I listened. Sometimes I questioned, but rarely. I was content to take of the heavenly manna as it was given me. With a heart full of gratitude and love.[1]

The Uncommon Possibilities

One day while researching in the archives of a Christian publishing company, I discovered a small volume published by that organization more than a century ago. I'm intrigued by old books. The cultural changes they reveal interest me, and the yellowed pages make me hope a curious someone will find my books in a library one hundred years from now. But neither of these factors attracted me to this book. The title appeared in a foreign language, but the subtitle read *My Dream of Heaven.*

Inside, the author claimed that during a severe illness she dreamed of heaven, a place she could barely describe with words. "I submit this imperfect sketch of a most perfect vision," she wrote, and the preceding story unveils her first encounter with the resurrected Christ. I checked out the book, read it at home, and wondered, *Should I believe her story?* The depiction of a gentle Savior and heaven's beauty reflected Scripture and appealed to and comforted me. God revealed heaven's glories to the apostles Paul and John, so couldn't He still speak this way thousands of years later?

However, I didn't know anything about this woman. Was she reliable? (There have been fake fantasies about the afterlife.) Because I couldn't confirm anything about the author, I had to suspend my belief, waiting until I enter the beautiful gates and look around myself. In the meantime, I now own a copy of the book to remind me of heaven's wonderful hope.

Similarly, when we listen for God's voice, we can anticipate the extraordinary possibilities, the mysterious ways He might speak to us. These approaches may occur less frequently, and they require careful discernment, but they capture our faith. For when heaven comes calling with the extraordinary, the Voice is so clear and indelible we can't deny that God is with us.

Preacher Calvin Miller explains that when God speaks through the extraordinary, He can captivate the most skeptical. "Saul once smirked over superstitious Christians who believed in the resurrection. He no doubt thanked God that he had been to the Jewish seminary and recognized primitive religion when he saw it," writes Miller. "Then all of a sudden he was confronted by a desert specter and found himself asking, 'Who is it?' Paul had to deal with a phenomenon he had already decided not to believe in. When the Christ of the Damascus Road said, 'I am Jesus of Nazareth,' Paul did not have the audacity to say, 'But you're in the graveyard; I've been telling everyone about it.'"[2] He listened and obeyed the Voice that defied the norms of nature to speak to him.

If God speaks to us in uncommon ways, like Paul we desire to listen and obey. And like the woman who dreamed about heaven, it's as if we've "been lifted to a higher plane of existence, to have drunk deeper draughts from the fountain of all good." We have felt God's undeniable presence and know that He has spoken to us.

God in the Ordinary

How does God turn the ordinary into the extraordinary? Usually by speaking to us in a way we couldn't fabricate on our own, so only He could be the messenger. Often this requires a touch of the supernatural or using the natural world in a poignant or mystical way. God's acts of communication range from the simple to the sublime, and when we "hear" them, they can change our lives.

Take care, though, to understand this: If we haven't yet heard God's voice through His uncommon means, this doesn't automatically indicate we're spiritually immature. Our Maker, for His own mysterious reasons, chooses the communication channels to reach us. Always and solely, He asks us to focus on the journey. We are to fix our eyes on Jesus, the author and perfecter of our faith (Hebrews 12:2), not on

the miraculous. Then as we grow in companionship with Him, following behind on the path He forges, stepping into His footprints, we
may walk into His wonder.

Often we begin experiencing God's wondrous means of communication through the common and physical aspects of our lives, the
things we can touch with our hands and see with wide-awake eyes.
And they are stimulating places to start.

❦ *The glory of nature.* "The heavens declare the glory of God; the
skies proclaim the work of his hands. Day after day they pour forth
speech; night after night they display knowledge. There is no speech or
language where their voice is not heard" (Psalm 19:1–3). Cicero, the
Roman orator and statesman, said, "The celestial order and the beauty
of the universe compel me to admit that there is some excellent and
eternal Being, who deserves the respect and homage of men."[3] Nature's
magnificence has always declared the glory of God and drawn people to
Him, but it also profoundly speaks through its minutia and simplicity.

"I've long felt a kinship with bugs, but there was one day when
that link became especially significant for me," explains a mother and
a gardener.

"When I was about eight months pregnant with our first son, a
bumblebee landed on my stomach. I shook him off, and not thinking
much more about it, I filed the incident away in my memory.

"Two years later, while pregnant with our second son, a big, red
wasp flew onto my pregnant belly. Again, I shook it off, though
admittedly with a great sense of urgency, as wasps are easily provoked.

"Four years later, when I was pregnant with our third child, a butterfly came to light on my rotund womb. Immediately, the bee and wasp incidents were relived: two stingers and a butterfly. At that moment I was sure that after two boys, our third child would be a girl. And I was right.

"Some may laugh at me for seeing these events as a personal message from God, but I don't mind. As that butterfly flew away, I knew better than ever that God is indeed very personal, and I should never underestimate His ways."[4]

We may feel uncomfortable with this woman's assessment, but at the same time, we can't discount the power of God's creation and creatures to speak to us. A friend of mine keeps notes about the biblical lessons she learns from her cat's behavior. Another friend, when she's feeling spiritually dry, hops in her sports utility vehicle and drives to the mountains. "I hike on the trails and soak in the beauty. Then, finally, I can hear God's voice," she explains. Working in my flower garden, I feel God's presence and observe the spiritual parallels between tilling the earth and cultivating spiritual growth—and sometimes the answers to problems unearth along with the worms and weeds.

From a tiny drop of water to the roaring of the sea, from the loose speck of earth to a mountain's massive solidity—God's Spirit can use any of His creation to speak to humanity. But will we cease striving long enough to listen? In "God's Grandeur" the poet Gerard Manley Hopkins wrote:

The world is charged with the grandeur of God.
It will flame out, like shining from shook foil;

It gathers to greatness, like the ooze of oil
Crushed. Why do men then now not reck his rod?
Generations have trod, have trod, have trod;
And all is seared with trade; bleared and smeared with
    toil;
And wears man's smudge and shares man's smell: the
    soil
Is bare now, nor can foot feel, being shod.

And for all this, nature is never spent;
There lives the dearest freshness deep down things;
And though the last lights off the black West went
Oh, morning, at the brown brink eastward, springs—
Because the Holy Ghost over the bent
World broods with warm breast and with ah!
bright wings.[5]

To both the Christian and the unbeliever, God's Spirit speaks through nature, if only we'll cock our heads and hear.

❦ *The "coincidence" of circumstances.* "I will lead the blind by ways they have not known, along unfamiliar paths I will guide them; I will turn the darkness into light before them and make the rough places smooth. These are the things I will do; I will not forsake them" (Isaiah 42:16). Sometimes when we're not looking for guidance God arranges events with His fingerprints all over them. The circumstances align so precisely we can't call them coincidental, and we know we're to take action. I'm watching one of those situations now. My mother, who lives several hundred miles away from me, has been contemplating a move from one town to another, and I hadn't planned on the transition happening for another year (as if I'm the one to direct her path!). In the last few days, though, circumstances have lined up as if to say, "Go now!" So she's planning and praying about financing a quick relocation.

Watching the unfolding details, supplied by God's intervention, builds my faith to pray for Mom's money needs. I believe when God manages the circumstances, He provides the resources to walk along unfamiliar paths, and when He extends His hand of guidance, He acts quickly and efficiently. And really, I shouldn't be surprised by the sudden move. For several months an "inner knowing" and human messengers have suggested to me that a change was approaching.

In my mother's life, God is using circumstances to put her on His path. At points in my life, He's used circumstances to pull me off a dangerous road. During my years away from God, a dermatologist diagnosed a mole on my upper right arm as malignant melanoma, a deadly form of cancer, and sent me directly to a surgeon. Within hours I landed in the hospital, and the next morning orderlies rolled me into surgery.

"You're OK; we got it all," someone said as I struggled awake in the recovery room. That night in a hospital bed, I knew God was demanding my attention through the frightening circumstances. *God is speaking to me,* I thought. *He wants me to come back to Him.* Just as the surgeon's knife cut into my arm, God was slicing through the barriers I'd erected toward Him.

It took a few more years before I fully returned to God, but during that interim the surgery's scar spoke of God's warning ("Your life could end") and mercy ("I saved you from death"). For twenty-five years I've had no reoccurrence, and the concave and irregular mark on my arm still silently speaks to me. I know that God wants me on the earth and that He'll never forsake me. In a tangible way, I am marked with God's love.

His Extraordinary Ways

"To the true disciple a miracle only manifests the power and love which are silently at work everywhere, as divinely in the gift of daily bread as in the miraculous multiplications of the loaves."[6]

This is a wise insight, one to remember as we assess the uncommon means God employs to speak to us. When intermittently we hear His voice through the extraordinary, we needn't think of these incidents as better or unusual or suspicious but as a natural part of the spiritual continuum He utilizes to communicate with humanity.

❦ *Visitations from angels.* "For he will command his angels concerning you to guard you in all your ways; they will lift you up in their hands, so that you will not strike your foot against a stone" (Psalm 91:11–12). In recent years there has been much ado about angels, and I've paid little attention. I believe in angels—that they are biblical and can visit us—but I haven't thought about them intersecting my life. Then several months ago my mother called and admitted hesitantly, "This morning as I woke up, I saw an angel."

"An angel?" I questioned. "Are you sure?"

"Yes."

"What did it look like?"

"He was at the foot of my bed, wearing a flowing gown."

Supernatural claims aren't the norm for my mother, so I sensed the visitation could have been "the real thing" from God.

"Did he say anything?" I asked, feeling a bit surreal.

"No, but he was standing in front of a door." My mother paused. "What do you think that means?"

A door? I panicked. If God was preparing to take Mom into eternity, I wasn't ready.

"I don't know, Mom. It could be some kind of transition. He might be telling you about a door you're going to walk through."

"Do you think it might be the door to heaven?"

Feeling anxious, I replied, "Well, if it is, tell him you're not ready. If he comes back, say you can't go there yet. I need you here."

"OK," she said quietly, knowing how much I dread losing her someday. "But I wonder what it means."

After that conversation I borrowed a friend's biblically based books about angels and pored over them. One of the books in particular calmed me down. It said God can send angels to inform us of coming changes and to say He'll be with us in the transition. Now that my mother is moving, the angel in her bedroom makes sense.

"Mom, remember the angel in your room?" I asked her yesterday. "I think he was telling you about this move. God is telling you not to be afraid, that He is with you as you walk through this doorway." She agreed.

I've always been deeply touched by God's tender care of my widowed mother. Because Mom's health is precarious, relocation feels daunting. So along with His messages through Scripture, circumstances, and friends, it seems He may have sent an angel as a finishing touch. That brief visit has reassured us.

Reassurance is much of the angels' role in relationship to Christians. In the spiritual realm, they guide, protect, comfort, and wage warfare for us. Occasionally they pull back the veil between the physical and eternal to speak, albeit silently, God's words of welfare and warning. "The Master is here," they say. "Stay close to Him and you will be safe."

❦ *Divinely appointed dreams.* "And afterward, I will pour out my Spirit on all people. Your sons and daughters will prophesy, your old men will dream dreams..." (Joel 2:28). We dream every night, yet sometimes an image or episode is so aligned with how God is speaking to us in the daytime, or it is so insightful and life changing, we wonder if it's a message from Him.

In their book *Windows of the Soul,* Drs. Paul Meier and Robert Wise state that these can be our most powerful and memorable dreams and we sometimes "are aware of being directly addressed by the divine."[7] They suggest that such messages may be from the Holy Spirit and can present instruction, clarification, direction, or discernment.

Dr. Meier describes a time when his youngest daughter ran away from home and sought help from a Christian counselor. She was depressed because her father was overly critical. The counselor asked Paul to attend a Saturday morning counseling session with his daughter. He agreed but felt angry. "After all, I am a psychiatrist!" he said. "What could some half-baked counselor tell me about what I might be contributing to my daughter's depression? After all, I had written books on how to raise children correctly!"

Early Saturday morning Paul's sleep was invaded by a dream. "With great intensity, the heavenly Father brought before my mind a personalized passage of Scripture I had memorized years before: 'Why do you look at the speck in your [daughter's] eye, but do not consider the plank in your own eye? Or how can you say to your [daughter], "Let me remove the speck out of your eye"; and look, a plank is in your own eye? Hypocrite! First remove the plank from your own eye, and then you will see clearly to remove the speck out of your [daughter's] eye'" (Matthew 7:3–5, NKJV).

The next morning the counselor began their session by reading the same Bible verses. "I couldn't help myself. I began weeping aloud," recalled Paul. "He stopped reading and everyone looked at me in astonishment. In simple, straightforward terms, I told them the story of my dream. By the time I finished, we were all overwhelmed. Needless to say, the counseling session was a great success. With all due respect to the young man, God had already set things in motion by calling me in the night."[8]

Still, we must be careful not to search for God's direction in every dream; to do so would yield some bizarre messages He never intends

us to receive. But I believe there are those rare, special occasions—
especially when we are earnestly seeking Him—in which He uses a
dream to impress us with a Scripture verse or a direction in which we
should go. When He does, it can be quite poignant.

My life purpose is to "publish the glad tidings for women," and
through some of my dreams I believe God has repeated the symbol of
"feet" to speak to me about hindrances to my writing ministry. I wrote
about the first dream in *Designing a Woman's Life* but repeat it below
to give a context for the recent, second dream.

During a late afternoon nap I dreamed I was lying on
my stomach while a woman I recognized cleaned my
feet. I'd gone to junior high with Karen, who attended
church but didn't live as a Christian.

In the dream Karen showed me the heels of my
feet; each one had a hole bored into it. When I peered
into the holes, it horrified me to observe layers of
crusty, dead skin instead of vibrant flesh and blood.

"You should let the physician take care of your
feet," remarked Karen, and then I woke up.

Lying on the couch, I mentally reviewed the dream.
It disturbed me. I knew it meant something, but I
didn't know how to interpret it. Wanting clues, I
grabbed my Bible and looked up verses that mentioned
feet. This one stood out to me: "How beautiful on the
mountains are the feet of those who bring good news,

who proclaim peace, who bring good tidings, who proclaim salvation, who say to Zion, 'Your God reigns!'" (Isaiah 52:7).

The feet carry God's good news, I thought.

Then the telephone rang. When I told my friend on the line about the dream and the verse, she asked, "Judy, is there anything in your life that would bar you from reaching women? Anything that would keep you from taking the good news to women like Karen?"

I began to cry. "Yes," I said softly. "There's a specific sin in my life that I need to take care of."

We talked awhile longer, and after I hung up the phone, it all fell together. Karen represented the women God was calling me to reach, but I could not effectively carry the good news to them with this sin in my life. I needed to let Christ, the great Physician, abolish my sin and prepare my feet for ministry.9

For more than a year my business has dipped financially. A few times I've gone two months without income, and it has stretched my faith in God's provision. At the advice of friends I began praying against hindrances in the spiritual realm that could be affecting my finances. One night after a long discussion with a friend, I dreamed about looking at the sole of my foot. I saw a worm that had burrowed its way into the foot, about to escape completely into my body, so I grabbed it by the still visible tip and yanked it out. I also pulled out a long nail.

The next morning I was amazed that God had used the same metaphor with me as he had employed twelve years earlier. It seemed the worm represented the destroyer of my finances, and the nail, the pain it inflicted. I was pulling them out through prayer and the Holy Spirit's power. Since that dream a month ago I've received queries about participating in seven new creative projects, not including the books I've contracted for this year. More than half are jobs I didn't initiate. In my dream, with symbols I would immediately recognize, God clarified at least one underlying source of the financial drought.

❧ *Eyes-open visions.* "Your young men will see visions" (Joel 2:28). Dreams and visions are often lumped together, and the two are similar because they speak to us in symbolic images and carry similar objectives. However, unlike dreams, God speaks through visions when we're awake, and they're rarer in occurrence than our slumbering metaphors. We may receive His messages via a quick flash in our mind's eye or, in fewer cases, a longer narrative.

Years ago when I first moved away from my hometown, I felt lonely and feared whether I could adequately take care of myself. One evening while I was crying alone, an image flashed through my mind. In the vision I was curled up, sleeping in the palm of a big hand. Immediately these words came to mind: "in the shadow of his hand he hid me" (Isaiah 49:2), and I felt comforted and protected by the Father.

In contrast, the missionary Amy Carmichael described a detailed, prophetic vision that compelled her to reach people in India for Christ:

I could not go to sleep, so I lay awake and looked; and I saw, as it seemed, this:

...I stood on a grassy sward, and at my feet a precipice broke sheer down into infinite space. I looked, but saw no bottom; only cloud shapes, black and furiously coiled, and great shadow-shrouded hollows, and unfathomable depths. Back I drew, dizzy at the depth.

Then I saw forms of people moving single file along the grass. They were making for the edge. There was a woman with a baby in her arms and another little child holding on to her dress. She was on the very verge. Then I saw that she was blind. She lifted her foot for the next step...it trod air. She was over, and the children with her. Oh, the cry as they went over!

Then I saw more streams of people flowing from all quarters. All were blind, stone blind; all made straight for the precipice edge. There were shrieks as they suddenly knew themselves falling, and a tossing up of helpless arms, catching, clutching at empty air. But some went over quietly, and fell without a sound....

Then I saw that along the edge there were sentries

set at intervals. But the intervals were far too great; there were wide, unguarded gaps between. And over these gaps the people fell in their blindness, quite unwarned; and the green grass seemed blood-red to me, and the gulf yawned like the mouth of hell.

Then I saw, like a little picture of peace, a group of people under some trees, with their backs turned toward the gulf. They were making daisy chains. Sometimes when a piercing shriek cut the quiet air and reached them it disturbed them, and they thought it a rather vulgar noise. And if one of their number started up and wanted to go and do something to help, then all the others would pull that one down. "Why should you get so excited about it? You must wait for a definite call to go! You have not finished your daisy chains yet. It would be really selfish," they said, "to leave us to finish the work alone."...

Once a girl stood alone in her place [as a sentry], waving the people back; but her mother and other relations called, and reminded her that her furlough was due; she must not break the rules. And being tired and needing a change she had to go and rest for a while; but no one was sent to guard her gap, and over and over the people fell, like a waterfall of souls.

Once a child caught a tuft of grass that grew at the

very brink of the gulf; it clung convulsively, and it
called—but nobody seemed to hear. Then the roots of
the grass gave way, and with a cry the child went over,
its two little hands still holding tight to the torn-off
bunch of grass. And the little girl who longed to be
back in her gap thought she heard the little one cry, and
she sprang up and wanted to go; at which they reproved
her, reminding her that no one is necessary anywhere;
the gaps would be well taken care of, they knew. And
then they sang a hymn.

Then through the hymn came another sound like
the pain of a million broken hearts wrung out in one
full drop, one sob. And a horror of great darkness was
upon me, for I knew what it was—the Cry of the
Blood.

Then thundered a voice, the Voice of the Lord:
And he said, "What hast thou done? The voice of thy
brothers' blood crieth unto Me from the ground."

To the vision Amy added, "God forgive us! God arouse us! Shame
us out of our callousness! Shame us out of our sin!"[10] A prophetic
vision often elicits our response to God's heart for the world.

🕯 *Undeniable miracles.* "You are the God who performs miracles; you display your power among the peoples" (Psalm 77:14). In one
sense, everything about God being in relationship with mortals is a miracle, including each way He speaks to us. Through the infallible

Scriptures or mouths of messengers, the Holy in communication with humanity should not be taken lightly. However, there are poignant times when God speaks by performing the "impossible." He mends a broken marriage; He heals an incurable disease; He changes the weather; He provides finances through uncanny means; He delivers the abused, addicted, and demon possessed. He can disrupt any typical course of nature or human endeavor to speak to people, both believers and non-believers, with redemptive words that create doubtless faith in Him. A true miracle is undeniable; it can't help but bolster belief (John 6:26–30).

With faith and prayer we can ask God for miracles, but He also breaks through on His own initiative. Human wisdom can't predict what God will do or when He will do it. We are told to "just believe" (Mark 5:36) and listen when He speaks. Through miracles God can say, "Believe in Me" or "I am your provider" or "I healed you because there are still things for you to do on the earth" or simply, "I love you."

My friend Madalene told me this story about learning to believe in and ask for God's miracles. She began, "I'd always been suspicious of people who asked God to give them what they could earn for themselves. My husband, Harlan, and I believed that hard work and frugality, supported by prayer, was the only way to supply our material needs. But then God changed our minds.

"When our children were still at home and finances were tight, I read a book about asking God, in faith, for the things we need. The author challenged his readers to write down three items they needed, thank God that He's going to provide them, and sign and date the paper. Oh yes, he also advised us to give God a deadline for supplying those needs and to thank Him each day for doing it."

She smiled and then continued: "At first I couldn't believe someone would be so bold, but then after re-reading the chapter I thought,
Why not? What have I got to lose? I jotted down three items, and I
remember trembling when I wrote these words: a car. Our old vehicle
wasn't safe anymore, and my husband often drove it long distances for
his work. I knew we really needed a car—it wasn't just a selfish
desire—but still, in my world a car was a big thing to ask for.

"The next morning at breakfast I told Harlan about my piece of
paper and that God was going to give us a car.

"'Are you crazy? You can't ask God to do that,' he sputtered and
insisted that I'd been presumptuous.

"'Let's just wait and see,' I said, trying to stay calm. 'I'll just continue to thank Him, and we'll see what happens.'

"He rolled his eyes and cast me a look that said, *This time, you're
off your rocker.*"

Madalene paused again, this time for dramatic effect, and finished
the story: "After that encounter I prayed each day, thanking God for
my three items, but the car occupied my mind the most.

"In the first month nothing happened. I didn't receive anything on
my list. The second month, nothing happened either. I kept praying
and thanking God but wondered if my husband was right. Then one
day toward the end of the third month, a man from our church called
and explained, 'Madalene, a group of us have so benefited from your
husband's ministry to us that we want to bless him with a gift.'

"'What's the gift?' I asked.

"It was not only a car but a brand new car! He told me to bring Harlan to a certain dealership and pick out any automobile we wanted. It would be paid for by our friends. These people had no idea I'd been thanking God for a car; they just thought we could use a new one.

"'Now you come with Harlan,' the man cautioned. 'If you don't, he'll pick out the cheapest car on the lot. We want you to insist on selecting a well-built model with all of the extras.' And that's what we did, thanking God on our way home from the car lot."

On the other hand, Janet learned that God can perform miracles even if we don't spread out the specifics. Not long after accepting Christ, she discovered termites underneath her old home, and an exterminator confirmed it'd take "major work" to eradicate them. "Oh, God," prayed Janet, "I can't afford this. I'm a single mother, struggling as it is. Please help me." When the bug expert came back with a plan of action, he checked under the house again. The termites were gone. Needless to say, Janet's faith in God's provision took a leap. She understands that with God nothing is impossible.

Helping Our Belief

With any of God's communication methods we are susceptible to deception, but perhaps more so with the extraordinary. Satan has armies of evil angels (Matthew 25:41), conniving people can fabricate stories, and earnest believers might claim they've heard God's voice but be mistaken. So when we think we're hearing God through the extra-ordinary, we can remember these guidelines:

❦ *First,* when God speaks through uncommon means, He stays true to the reliable characteristics of His voice, discussed in chapter 4. He especially doesn't lead us into sin, contradict Scripture, or destroy lives.

❦ *Second,* God's extraordinary messages stand the tests of confirmation and authentication. His uncommon methods usually don't stand in isolation. They synchronize thematically with messages in His Word, the advice of confidants, the inner impressions of the soul that already exist, requests for confirmation, the test of time. And if needed, His miracles like healing can stand up to a doctor's scrutiny.

❦ *Third,* if we're defensive about explaining or justifying the extraordinary message or if we're compulsive about pursuing it, we may not have heard from God. He is a steady light, recognizable by godly people around us. A light we're not to hide under a bushel but to let shine so people will "praise your Father in heaven" (Matthew 5:16). If we have truly heard from God, it's important to tell our story. It builds our faith and the belief of those around us—and it gives God the glory.

Several people at my church had warned one of the pastors about a suspicious-looking mole on his face. He prayed that God would heal it, and before his appointment with a doctor came due, the mole dried up and fell off. He told us about the incident at last week's service, and people gasped, then applauded and praised God. It's difficult to deny an episode like that: The mole was there; now it's gone, without the marks of a scalpel. It's even harder to dissuade the man who held the crumbled bits in his hand. He believes.

And that is the underlying purpose of all of God's communication. Whenever He speaks, He wants to hear us reply, "I do believe; help me overcome my unbelief!" (Mark 9:24). Especially when we hit walls of silence, and need to break down barriers to hearing His voice.

Chapter Seven

Breaking Down
the Barriers

*Your enemy is the deceiver of the world
and the accuser of the brethren,
accusing them day and night.
So don't listen to him!
He's a Tokyo Rose of the worst sort.*

KAY ARTHUR

It was a nightmare. Truly, a nightmare. Except unfortunately I was awake, sitting in a hotel room late at night, alone and terrified.

How could this be happening to me? I asked myself repeatedly. In the last few days my anxiety had ballooned from menacing to paralyzing, and I barely recognized myself. I felt as if I'd gotten trapped in an exceptionally bad B movie, playing the part of the distressed heroine with no imminent rescuer in sight. *If I get through this mess alive, I'm never speaking at a conference again,* I vowed. And I meant it. Truly, I meant it.

Several months before this moment of madness I'd been asked to speak at a Christian women's retreat. While I usually speak to groups of fifty or less, this weekend I'd face a crowd of five hundred. More daunting, however, was the lineup of speakers. To this day I'm not sure why the conference director invited me, because I was a virtually unknown speaker sandwiched between two well-known and entertaining women—the type who, with a few clever stories, can induce an audience to laugh, lament, and learn all at once.

I am a writer, not a polished speaker like these women, I had thought. But I'd felt flattered by the invitation and had said yes.

I'd been assigned a topic I knew intimately: finding your mission in life. I'd written both a book and Bible study about it and had spoken to groups about pursuing your purpose with passion. But for this conference I was transitioning from small-group teacher to a featured speaker, and I wanted a fresh revelation from God for my message. As the months turned into weeks and then days before the conference, though, my work life grew busier and more stressful, and I didn't write my speech.

Finally a week before the conference I settled down to develop it. Legal pad and pen in hand, I searched my brain for an arresting introduction—and then it happened. My mind went blank. Totally blank. My brain felt as hollow as a dried-up gourd. No ideas. No anecdotes. Not even a few shriveled seeds rattling around in the space. And especially not "a word from the Lord."

Okay, I can get through this, I told myself. *It's simply a matter of timing. I'll pray, and tomorrow the words will flow.*

The next day the only "flow" was the fear seeping into my head. I skipped a day, then tried again. Nothing.

I called friends and asked for prayer. I petitioned God myself, and each day was the same. By then a full-blown paralysis had gripped me. I cried intermittently and pleaded continually with my brain, but it ignored me, deep in a dormancy from which it might not recover. For me, the prospect of standing in front of a large group and winging it was unacceptable and horrifying.

By now the words "You Will Fail" took residence where my brain used to live. I felt incompetent, out of my league, and desperate. I hoped for illness to strike me so I could stay home. At the conference not only would I fail, I would flop in front of polished professionals I wanted to impress, in front of women who had paid to attend this conference, in front of ministry leaders who could invite me to speak at their events.

The day I left for the conference, annoyingly healthy but mentally frozen, the stakes loomed so high I wanted to vomit. Instead, I climbed the stairs to the airplane cabin, carrying a briefcase with no speech inside. *Why hadn't God answered my pleas for help? What had happened to hearing His "fresh word" for these women? Where in the world was He?*

As I buckled up for the Friday flight, inching toward failure, I tried not to think. I fell asleep and dreamed of the humiliation ahead.

Nobody at the hotel knew about my crisis. How do you tell a conference director, an accomplished speaker herself, that you're about to bomb her perfectly arranged weekend? How can you admit to women you've just met that you're an impostor, an unprepared interloper who should be shot immediately and relieved of her misery?

Late in the afternoon of the first day, the speakers gathered in a hospitality room to get acquainted and chat. Most of the speakers had attended this conference before and loved it. Sitting in a circle on plush chairs and couches, everyone else appeared calm and anticipatory. I felt dreadful. The director eventually said, "Why don't we introduce ourselves and give a short overview of what we'll be talking about? We can practice the introductions we're giving in front of the audience tonight. Judy, why don't you begin?"

I mumbled something about "being here for the first time" and not knowing what she expected. Could someone else begin? I gave her my best smile.

"That's fine," she said cheerily, and while the others rattled off their finely tuned preambles, I quickly made up something in my head. When my turn rolled around again, I stumbled through it, and as soon as the meeting ended, I slid out the door. An enormous clock was ticking—no, *clanging*—inside my head, right next to the "You Will Fail" sign. I fled to my room again, pulled out a notepad, and wrote down nothing.

I picked up the phone, dialed a friend's number, and choking with sobs, asked her to call my prayer team. I needed them on their knees, begging God to help me. *"This is an emergency!"* I cried.

"It certainly is," she reassured me, "but God can get you through it."

"How is He going to do *that?*" I countered. "He's on vacation somewhere."

"He will," she said. "I'll call everybody to pray," she added, and we hung up.

And still, nothing.

That evening after dinner I lined up with the speakers to introduce ourselves and our topics. The first two women, both famous and funny, delighted and charged up the audience. Somehow I managed to ride their wake and introduce myself to the sea of eager faces, quickly improvising. After this, I stood in the back of the auditorium for ten minutes of the first speaker's presentation. She looked great, sounded even better, kept the crowd roaring, and my stomach churned.

I exited, and sapped of energy from not eating all day, I began the torturous walk back to a silent room.

❦

It was 11:00 P.M. I was sitting in a hardback chair, fighting sleep, when the phone rang.

"Judy, this is Nancy. What's happening out there?"

My dear, committed friend Nancy. Always there for me, no matter the mess I'm in.

"I can't do this!" I wailed. "I'm hungry and exhausted. I can't think of what to say. And I'm on the platform tomorrow morning at ten o'clock. Please come get me!"

"You can do this. I know you can," she countered. "I'm going to talk you through it." Then she reminded me that I knew this topic well, that I could trust the creative process within me, that above all I could depend on God to undergird me, even in this situation.

"When you get up to speak, God will take over," she explained.

"But what am I going to say? I have nothing new to say!"

"You don't need anything new to say," she said. "Talk about what you already know. Talk about what's in your book. Tell them what God has already taught you about purpose. Believe in your passion."

After our conversation I pulled out my book, flipped through it, and fretted for a few more hours. Around two in the morning I finally decided this was it. *Do or die,* I thought and began writing. I wrote an introduction based on a story my manicurist had told me the week before. Then I opened the book I'd written and haltingly created an outline by plagiarizing my own work. I copied the "same old" principles, the "same old" anecdotes and applications from the book. *They're familiar to me, but maybe they'll be fresh to this audience,* I consoled myself. Around five o'clock I jotted down a conclusion and rolled into bed, both setting the alarm clock and requesting a wake-up call for a few hours later.

There's nothing more I can do, I thought. I covered myself head to toe with the comforter and fell asleep instantly.

❦

I arrived in the auditorium a half-hour before my speech, privately repeating Nancy's advice as a litany: *God will take over. God will take over. God will take over.* After getting fitted for a portable mike, a new acquaintance grabbed me and whispered, "Be fearless!" and I walked toward the podium. She had no idea what those words meant to me at that moment.

"Good morning," I said to the audience, and Nancy was right. At that moment *God did take over*. My mind was clear. I could remember my stories. I managed to move enough to write principles on the overhead projector. Women took notes and laughed in the right places. About every ten minutes I felt like stopping and sitting down, but I kept going for an hour. I wasn't the best speaker that weekend, but God still used me. I talked about the pleasure and pain of purpose, about the ups and downs of my own experiences, and tears filled a few eyes.

Relieved to finish, I barely heard the applause as I stepped down from the platform, ready to run back upstairs. The security of my room, however, was not an option. Women invaded me and my book table, crying, complimenting, purchasing my books, and requesting autographs.

"Your speech meant so much to me."

"You hit me right where I live."

"You gave us spiritual meat."

"You've given me the courage to pursue my dream."

"Thank you for letting God speak through you."

The positive comments continued throughout the weekend, and I received cards and letters from participants over the next month. It wasn't until I returned home, however, that I fully realized what had happened. God had created a miracle. He *had* spoken to me and to those women. And once again, I cried.

The Ways of Warfare

Though it happened a year ago, something inside me still cringes while telling this near-miss story. It's uncomfortable admitting to the audacity of showing up at a conference without a speech. However, the foolishness of overlooking spiritual warfare was my biggest mistake related to that weekend, particularly in striving to hear from God.

In the thick of our lives—from dashing around with responsibilities to managing our inner emotions—we forget the evil spirit world's impact on us. I certainly did. I thought my brain emptied out because of a personal character flaw (and I have many) or that God had failed me. I struggle with procrastination, and I understand that if we don't wait on God, it's difficult to hear from Him (I was guilty of both). But I also now realize that with old-fashioned spiritual warfare, I could have erased much of my difficulty. I'd been attacked by fear, which originates with Satan, and failed to appropriate what I knew about battling unseen but nonetheless terrorizing spiritual forces.

If we're to consistently hear from God, we need to break down the barriers these forces build to block out His communication with us. This begins with believing in their existence and learning how they operate—not to give the evil spirit world more credit than it deserves, but to effectively tumble their efforts to defeat us.

"There are two equal and opposite errors into which our race can fall about the devils," wrote C. S. Lewis. "One is to disbelieve in their existence. The other is to believe, and to feel an excessive and unhealthy interest in them."[1] As Christ's followers, many of us live somewhere between these two extremes but still don't incorporate the truth of spiritual warfare. We don't subscribe to the "demons in every door-knob" theology, yet we often don't believe enough. Because of fear, a lack of knowledge, a veneer of sophistication, or merely inattention, we allow Satan and his armies to rob us of hearing from God. If we aren't alert, we can attribute our problems to emotional downturns or per-plexing circumstances created by ourselves or others, when the core source is spiritual evil—the enemy using our emotions or relationships or circumstances to harass and discourage us, clogging our spiritual ears.

The devil is a subtle deceiver, and unless we awaken to the ways of spiritual warfare, we'll mislabel his tactics. He doesn't brandish a pitch-fork and announce his presence. Though he's capable of outrageous acts, he frequently attacks us through our vulnerabilities. If we're prone to anger, depression, control, criticism, fear, pride, self-pity, worry, or whatever, he'll tempt and oppress us through those weaknesses. He sears us through specific attitudes, propensities, and recurring sins, causing us to think, *It's just me,* when actually, we're surrounded by his menacing troops.

At the same time, Satan will eventually "show his hand" like a foolish card player. Telltale characteristics announce his activity:

❦ *negative thoughts and emotions about specific matters or a general sense of despair, hopelessness, or unworthiness* (Though I have speaking skills, I didn't feel capable of addressing a large group and gave in to fear and despair.)

❦ *an intensity of emotion or opinion that is extreme and out of proportion to the circumstances* (The fear debilitated me.)

🦌 *a path that leads to strife, addiction, destruction, or isolation* (Though I was headed toward disaster, for a while I hid my feelings from people out of concern for what they might think.)

🦌 *accusatory thoughts or words about ourselves, others, or God* (A You Will Fail sign emerged in my head.)

🦌 *an inability to trust or relate to God* (I couldn't find or hear God and accused Him of taking a vacation from me.)

🦌 *confusion, unclear thinking, or mental and emotional paralysis* (I couldn't think. The more I tried, the more the paralysis increased and the confusion thickened.)

🦌 *physical problems* (The anxiety kicked into my back, causing pain.)

Now let me be clear. There are other factors that cause some of these problems, such as genetics, exhaustion, inner wounds, or immaturity, so this list is not absolute. We must learn to wage spiritual warfare ourselves, discerning the difference between demonic activity and other factors.

Satan also works in many ways, so the list is not definitive, either. Every Christian could develop a list unique to his or her personality and circumstances. However, if one or more of these characteristics hover and harangue, it's wise to check for a devilish presence. (I experienced them all, but not all are necessary to suspect Satan's influence.)

"Jesus completed the work the Father gave him to do on earth, and the enemy can do nothing to change the perfect plan of salvation. But Satan *does* keep people from hearing the message; he also distorts and misrepresents the message. In other words, he vents his rage against the

Father by taking vengeance on us. Satan tries to prevent our deliverance and keeps us alienated from God, knowing this frustrates God's desire to see us reconciled to Himself," explain Quin Sherrer and Ruthanne Garlock, speakers and authors devoted to teaching spiritual warfare principles.[2] Satan not only muddles hearing the good news of God's salvation, but he keeps believers from God's redemptive messages for their lives and outreach in the world. He likes to preoccupy and paralyze—or do anything to keep us spiritually off track, confused, and hopeless.

The Name and the Blood

If we can't hear from God, and we suspect the evil spirit world's presence, what can we do? "We then must oppose the spirits of darkness which blind and deceive the minds of the hearers," continue Sherrer and Garlock. "We must also resist evil forces trying to hinder our reaching people with the gospel. Our goal is to see men and women—believers and unbelievers—set free from the bondage of Satan by the power of the blood of Jesus."[3]

This blood is more powerful than satanic forces, and when we resist the devil and his supporters in the name of Jesus, claiming His blood as our covering, they will flee. Scriptures indicate they *must* flee; they can't stand against the Holy Name and the humiliation of a guaranteed loss. James 4:7 declares, "Submit yourselves, then, to God. Resist the devil, and he will flee from you." Hebrews 2:14–15 explains that Jesus "shared in [our] humanity so that by his death he might destroy him who holds the power of death—that is, the devil—and free those who all their lives were held in slavery by their fear of death."

For most of us, resisting the devil in everyday life is a simpler process than we may think. We can speak to him, saying, "I resist you, Satan. Be gone in the name of Jesus." We can then ask Jesus to cover and protect us with His blood. Because there are also many evil spirits, assigned different menacing jobs, we may also resist specific demons—fear, oppression, etc.—based on what manifests itself in the situation. When I remember to practice it, this basic warfare often banishes oppressive thoughts, helps to crumble barriers in relationships, or alters hindering circumstances. Peace and joy replace doubt and hopelessness, and I sense God's presence and communication with me.

Of course, there are demonic strongholds that need repeated prayer and fasting and numbers of Christians railing against them in Jesus' name, but for many there is remarkable victory in simply the name and blood of Jesus. We gain even more power if we pray with another person or a small gathering, for Jesus promises, "Again, I tell you that if two of you on earth agree about anything you ask for, it will be done for you by my Father in heaven. For where two or three come together in my name, there am I with them" (Matthew 18:19—20). The key is assertively waging war rather than passively resigning to the circumstances. Thankfully, in their homes miles away, a few praying women waged this warfare for me as I sat alone in a hotel room last year, and I was set free to hear God's voice through Nancy.

Since that terrorizing weekend I've purposed to grow more aware of spiritual warfare and my authority, in Jesus' name, over its havoc. I still can lethargically think "it's just me," but when I've applied the name and the blood, I've brushed the hem of the miraculous. A poignant incident occurred just last week as I worked on this book. Concerned about finances, I felt disheartened when a promised pay-check didn't arrive in the mail. Into the evening I felt sadder and sadder until I began crying and couldn't stop. I cried on and off for three days, unable to speak on the phone without surrendering to sobs. I couldn't write much, and I felt alone and hopeless about my monetary and pro-fessional future. God seemed far away and His voice nonexistent. Finally out of desperation I called two friends to stop by the house after work and pray for me.

After my friends interceded for me, they suggested I anoint with oil a bedroom where they sensed oppression and rebuke Satan. (In Exodus 40:9 the Lord told Moses to anoint the tabernacle with oil to consecrate it for holiness.) They also said playing praise tapes would aid the enemy's departure. (In 2 Samuel 22:4 David sang, "I call to the LORD, who is worthy of praise, and I am saved from my enemies.") Then my friends said good-bye, leaving me to do the job alone.

I can't do this by myself, I thought. *It's scary.* But within a few moments I answered: *If it will clear this awful depression, I'll do it. And besides, the name of Jesus is more powerful than anything here.*

With that, I grabbed a bottle of olive oil, a portable tape deck, and the only Christian tape I own. Upstairs in a bedroom I switched on the tape and sang along, praising God. Then I dabbed oil on a door-post and rebuked Satan, depression, oppression, and other hindering spirits that came to mind. Not only did I feel a lightening in the room's atmosphere, but the depression and hurt lifted off me, as though a heavenly hand had sutured the inner wound without a scar's trace. I filled with joy, laughter, and a peace that, given my financial circumstances, didn't make sense, except for the Holy Spirit's fullness. I changed into pajamas, fell into bed, and slept through the night.

However, before I dozed off, I suddenly thought about two small Indian statues owned by my landlord and probably carted home from her many travels. They sat on a shelf in the basement. *Why would they come to mind?* The next morning I called my friends to confer. They said yes, spirits can accompany the religious artifacts of pagan societies. There could be more hindering spirits in the basement. I descended the stairs and repeated my oil-and-praise tape procedure, resisting evils lurking in the house. I also anointed the statues and pled the blood of Jesus over my home. After this I bounded upstairs, and the Holy Spirit's presence was so strong I basked in joy for two more days. Once again, I could hear His voice.

If I hadn't experienced the episode myself, I might consider it fanatical. But the radical difference in my disposition convinced me again of the spirit world's reality and Satan's determination to destroy our relationship and communication with God. I also remembered that each time I write a book, it comes under spiritual attack. The activity may vary, but always it is potent. Still, Jesus' name is holy and powerful, and when we use it, we will marvel. It's not coincidental that a few days after this incident my immediate financial needs were provided for unexpectedly.

Practicing What We Know

We don't need to wait until the enemy hits and God's voice grows dim to practice spiritual warfare. The Bible tells us to guard against attacks, particularly by wearing the armor of God. Paul told the Ephesian church, "Put on the full armor of God so that you can take your stand against the devil's schemes. For our struggle is not against flesh and blood, but against the rulers, against the authorities, against the powers of this dark world and against the spiritual forces of evil in the heavenly realms. Therefore put on the full armor of God, so that when the day of evil comes, you may be able to stand your ground, and after you have done everything, to stand" (6:11–13). This armor includes:

❦ *"the belt of truth buckled around your waist"* (verse 14). We infiltrate our souls with God's truth, acknowledging who we are in Christ and insisting on truthfulness in our "inner parts" (Psalm 51:6) and relationships.

❦ *"the breastplate of righteousness"* (verse 14). We forsake sin and its temptations, renewing ourselves with God's morality. We follow His ways.

❦ *"feet fitted with the readiness that comes from the gospel of peace"* (verse 15). We avoid strife and disunity, ushering peace into our hearts and relationships. Peace guards us in life's difficult circumstances.

❦ *"the shield of faith, with which you can extinguish all the flaming arrows of the evil one"* (verse 16). We believe in and appropriate God's promises to us. We exercise faith in His supernatural power to intervene in our lives.

❦ *"the helmet of salvation"* (verse 17). We remember our redemption and grasp the inheritance of God's children.

❦ *"the sword of the Spirit, which is the word of God"* (verse 17). We read, meditate, and apply the Scriptures to our lives. We obey God's Word expressed to humanity universally and to us personally.

In addition, we're to "pray in the Spirit on all occasions with all kinds of prayers and requests. With this in mind, be alert and always keep on praying for all the saints" (verse 18). Prayer builds up the inner person, strengthening the sinews of righteousness, and releases the heavenlies to battle unseen forces on our behalf. When Daniel of the Old Testament prayed to understand a vision, an angel finally appeared and explained, "Do not be afraid, Daniel. Since the first day that you set your mind to gain understanding and to humble yourself before your God, your words were heard, and I have come in response to them. But the prince of the Persian kingdom resisted me twenty-one days. Then Michael, one of the chief princes, came to help me, because I was detained there with the king of Persia" (Daniel 10:12–13). When we're waiting to hear God's voice, we may be delayed because of the spiritual battle. For this reason alone, it's vital to persevere in prayer.

For many of us, advice about spiritual warfare is not new information. Our oversight is not practicing what we already know. However, if we're to keep the spiritual airwaves open for God's transmittals, we cannot overlook Satan's realm. Nor can we ignore sin.

Looking Within at Sin

When Rosalie's family sits down for an evening meal, an extravaganza begins. She spares no expense buying exotic food and cooking utensils to showcase her son's culinary abilities. In fact, Rosalie spares no expense for anything. She sports designer clothes for herself, a state-of-the-art computer for her daughter, an airplane for her husband, and whatever else she feels like charging to numerous credit cards and checking accounts.

An airplane? Maybe for a wealthy person's shopping list, but Rosalie isn't rich. She just spends lots of money, writes rubber checks, and never pays the bills. But somehow she always manages to obtain more credit, more money, more things. When her husband's paycheck advance isn't enough (and it never is), Rosalie alters the amount and cashes it at the bank. She empties her son's savings. When credit cards hit their maximum limits, she reports them as stolen so she doesn't have to pay the bills. When she wants even more spending power, she fakes her way into an enormous bank loan.

Rosalie maneuvers with such aplomb she never gets caught or pays for her transgressions. She recognizes her sins, though. Rosalie regularly visits her town's tiny Catholic church. She confesses her activities to the priest, asks for absolution, receives his forgiveness, and trots out to spend exorbitant sums again.

"Catholicism is a wonderful religion," she tells a houseguest one evening. "You admit your sins, and they're not sins anymore."

Rosalie's crowning performance begins when from her home

office she cracks the computers at her daughter's workplace. First, Rosalie only alters the amount of her daughter's paycheck, but then she pirates money from the company's accounts. All the while, she keeps confessing to the priest who eventually comes unglued. The priest listens to the scandalous admissions, but because of the confessional booth's confidentiality, he can't tell anyone or turn in Rosalie to the authorities.

"It's not enough to confess everything," the priest warns Rosalie. "You have to be sorry. Truly sorry." She doesn't follow his advice. When Rosalie tells the priest she's starting a multinational business to help people "beat the system" the way she does, he bangs his head against a wall after she leaves.

Sound unbelievable? It is. Rosalie lives in the film *Rosalie Goes Shopping*.[4] Among other lessons, the movie points to the futility of a faith that doesn't transform us personally. In the end Rosalie doesn't change because in the beginning she doesn't intend to. She uses confession to placate her conscience rather than repent of her sins. She's not interested in truly hearing from God.

However, Rosalie gets one thing right. She confesses her sins daily—and there is biblical precedence for talking to God that often. In Psalm 5:3 David told the Lord, "Every morning you hear my voice. Every morning, I tell you what I need, and I wait for your answer" (NCV). However, he also said, "If I had cherished sin in my heart, the Lord would not have listened" (Psalm 66:18), so confession affected those conversations too. We can learn from David's example. If we hide sin within, the Lord will not hear us, but neither can we hear Him.

A lack of true repentance diminishes His voice, either because we won't listen or He stops communicating.

When we sin, our relationship with God stymies. We begin avoiding time with Him. We may even start running, especially if, like Rosalie, we persist in sin we don't want to forsake. Or, we may be ignorant of unconfessed sin. Unaware of sin's ability to produce spiritual deafness, we may ask, "Why doesn't God speak to me? Why can't I hear Him?" We hit walls of silence in our Father-child relationship and don't understand why. Or, we can placate an attitude or behavior for so long we don't recognize it as sin anymore. Until we're desperate, we don't recognize that God hasn't spoken in a while.

Whatever the sin and however we've entertained it, God still loves and pursues us. He desires to forgive our transgressions and restore an intimate relationship with Him. Accordingly, He sets aside His guidance and confidences—the messages He longs to gently speak to us—and becomes the voice of conviction. Sometimes with whispers, sometimes with shouts, He points to sin and repentance. He wants to pull us back into His arms, place His cheek next to ours, and speak reassurances into our ears. If only we will acknowledge our sin and turn from it.

Our tendency, however, is to practice the Garden of Eden approach to sin. Once we're exposed, we hide from God's companionship, fearing His punishment. In my Bible the most marked-up book is Isaiah because it repeatedly insists that despite our waywardness God doesn't want us to suffer the serious consequences of sin. He is compassionate and forgives again and again. (I've often needed this reminder.) If we repent and follow Him, He will restore and even bless us, carrying us in His protective arms. It is our stubborn refusal to forsake sin that leads away from His voice, into destruction.

Isaiah 59 begins, "Surely the arm of the LORD is not too short to save, nor his ear too dull to hear. But your iniquities have separated you from your God" (verses 1–2). The Lord describes Israel's offenses, but when the people repent, He promises, "The Redeemer will come to Zion, to those in Jacob who repent of their sins.... My Spirit, who is on you, and my words that I have put in your mouth will not depart from your mouth" (verses 20–21). These are words of eternal love and redemption, and they're in our mouths because we've allowed God to speak them into our ears.

The evangelist Dwight L. Moody exclaimed, "How sweet our life will be, how pure our conscience will be, if God has forgiven everything, if we have brought everything to light, and turned from our sins, and the work has been deep and thorough!"5 How wonderful to once again hear His gentle voice.

Other Barriers to His Voice

Even though spiritual warfare and unconfessed sin largely affect our ability to hear God's voice, they aren't the only reasons we hit barriers. So also consider the following possibilities.

❦ *The barrier of busyness.* Frankly, we may be too busy to hear from God. Our culture emphasizes the word *rush,* and believers have joined in. We are overworked, overscheduled, overspent, and unable to cope. In contrast, communication with God requires time to pray, read and ponder Scripture, listen for His voice, and obey what He tells us. If we want to hear from God, we need to ask, "Am I too busy? What needs to change so I can take time to hear from God?"

"The only way to [answer this question] is to begin each day by relinquishing its hours to God and letting *Him* establish the balance between...marriage, family, career, and ministry," advises business-woman Mayo Mathers. To slow down her schedule, she prays Psalm 90:12: "Teach us to number our days and recognize how few they are; help us to spend them as we should" (TLB). Then she adds, "It's your schedule, God. Teach me to number my days."[6]

❦ *A call to completion.* Is there something God has asked you to do? Have you done it? Sometimes we don't hear from God because we haven't obeyed what He's already told us, or we need to "complete" an obedience, finishing a task. To disobey or partially obey is to sin. Also, we may not understand all of God's messages—all of His working in our lives—until we obey.

"If we hold back our obedience...we shall be disobedient," explains former missionary Elisabeth Elliot. "There are truths that cannot be known except by doing them. The Gospels show many cases of those who wish to understand rather than to obey. Jesus had scathing words for them. On one occasion He turned from them to those who had already believed in Him, and said, 'If you dwell within the revelation I have brought, you are indeed my disciples; you shall know the truth, and the truth shall set you free.' To 'dwell within the revelation' surely means living by what we have been shown. It means hearing and doing."[7]

❦ *Our internal injuries.* Inner wounds can cut so deep that the emotional pain interferes with our ability to hear from God, even our desire to hear from Him. For example, if we suffered at the hands of an abusive father, we can mistakenly think the heavenly Father is untrustworthy and punitive. Or perhaps we've been so disappointed we blame God for letting us down. Or, if Christians hurt us, it's difficult separating their actions from God's intentions. Whatever the hurt, we can bring it to Christ's cross for healing, for "by his wounds we are healed" (Isaiah 53:5). But to do so, it's mandatory to give up self-pity, forgive the offenders, abandon bitterness, and stop clutching the offense.

Some woundedness may also be inflicted from generational sins, the iniquities and pain passed through our families. "Although I believe we need to deal with today's issues and our own sin problems, it is also important to consider the sins of the fathers," advises Cindy Jacobs, who frequently teaches about hearing from God. "I have seen people who have family histories of sexual sin or addiction become victimized again and again, even after receiving counseling, as a result of the legal right Satan has to hurt them through the generational sins of their fathers.... This right must be taken away through prayer, confession, and repentance."[8]

❦ *The physical factors.* Sometimes our physical condition interferes with an ability to hear God. We may need to let pain, illness, depression, or exhaustion subside before we can hear His words. Getting enough sleep, caring for physical needs, or simply relaxing can be a spiritual act, clearing the barriers to communication. Beyond these, we may also need medical attention or personal counseling.

As a young woman I dumped my anxieties on an older friend, who replied, "Sometimes the most spiritual thing we can do is get enough sleep." She knew me well, and her comment, though perplexing at that moment, proved true. Pressed for time, I tended to stay up late to accomplish a task, skimping on sleep. Persisting in sleep deprivation then affected my relationship with God; He seemed to slip away, along with the hours of lost sleep. Through the years I've learned that adequate sleep keeps me more alert to God's voice within and to His speaking through people and circumstances.

Whenever we struggle to hear God, we can offer the problem to Him, asking if there is anything we need to do or any bondages that need to be broken, or whether we just need to wait to hear His voice. If we're puzzled about hearing God's voice, Cindy Jacobs suggests this prayer:

> Lord, I now give all of myself to You. Bring to light those
> things that would distort my hearing Your voice. Show
> me any place where I am bitter and wounded. Cleanse me
> with Your precious blood from all unrighteousness. Do
> whatever is necessary to make me a whole person. Cleanse
> me of the iniquities in the generations of my family.
> Cleanse me of sin in my own past and present. I now give
> You permission to deal with me so I can change, be
> healed, restored and set free from any bondages in my life.
> I now pray like David in Psalm 51:10 (NASB), "Create in
> me a clean heart, O God, and renew a steadfast spirit
> within me." In Jesus' name. Amen.[9]

The Ever-Working God

Could it be we haven't heard from God about a specific matter because He hasn't spoken yet? We can impatiently expect God to speak when we ask Him to, forgetting that His ways are not our ways, His timing is not our timing. God told Ezekiel, "I the LORD will speak what I will" (12:25) and accordingly, He speaks when He is ready. We cannot expedite His reply.

However, we can be assured of God's goodness and work on our behalf. If it's spiritual warfare, He battles with us. If we've sinned, He convicts us. If we're busy, He woos us back. If we overlook obedience, He warns and reminds us. If we're emotionally wounded or physically sick, He heals and restores. If we want guidance or a response to prayer, He answers us, whether it's yes, no, or wait.

David wrote, "I am still confident of this: I will see the goodness of the LORD in the land of the living. Wait for the LORD; be strong and take heart and wait for the LORD" (Psalm 27:13–14). To wait is not to hit a barrior. It is to believe in the goodness of God—a Father who honors the smallest of steps we take to hear Him.

Chapter Eight

Praise for Small Steps

The best way to handle failure is to know that it is forgivable.
I need never fear the anger of my Shepherd if I ask to try again.
I will find only His loving arms, tender touch,
and feast after all my failure.

JILL BRISCOE

The boy Samuel ministered before the LORD under Eli. In those days the word of the LORD was rare; there were not many visions.

One night Eli, whose eyes were becoming so weak that he could barely see, was lying down in his usual place. The lamp of God had not yet gone out, and Samuel was lying down in the temple of the LORD, where the ark of God was.[1]

Samuel missed his mother.

Lying in the semidarkness late at night, he thought about her last visit to the temple. Closing his eyes, the boy envisioned Hannah's face: the lilting smile, the dancing eyes, the mouth full of kisses for his curly-haired head. Squeezing his eyes tighter and pulling the blanket to his chin, he imagined his mother's embrace. She'd held him so tight he'd almost stopped breathing, but he didn't mind. Samuel loved her warmth, her smell, her engulfing presence. Every ounce of Hannah delighted in her son, and he knew that. He needed to know that. Living in the temple could be lonely for a boy whose father figure was an emotionally distant old priest.

So Samuel welcomed his mother's hugs, though other boys his age might have been embarrassed by the affection. Hannah's love had to last a long time—long enough to endure their many days of separation. After each glorious visit, full of simple gifts and elaborate stories of home, she'd return to their family in the hills. He'd stay behind in God's house, remembering his mother's words.

"Samuel, I love you so much, and I miss you with all my heart!" she'd exclaimed as she left, looking back over her shoulder. "Remember, you have important work to do for God, and He will watch over you while we're apart. You can trust Him, Samuel. You can put your faith in Him." Hannah's voice quavered, and she turned abruptly, hoping he hadn't detected her tears.

But Samuel had seen.

In bed he turned on his side, wiped away the trickles on his face, and watched the flickering lamp of God about to extinguish itself for the night. *God's house must be a place for tears,* he thought. In this temple Hannah had fallen to the floor, weeping and begging the Lord for a son.

"Then God gave me a miracle. He gave me you!" she'd told her toddler son years ago, gently tousling his hair. As a young boy, Samuel had heard the story many times, but he had never tired of it. "Tell me again about how much you wanted to have me for a son," he had said, and Hannah had laughed, sighed deeply, and reminisced again.

Jehovah must be wonderful, thought Samuel as he rolled onto his stomach. Why else would Mama have left him in the temple at such a young age? Why else would he have spent his childhood here? Why else would she feel proud of his job serving God by helping Eli?

But she said I would meet God. When will I see Him?

🖎

Then the LORD called Samuel.

Samuel answered, "Here I am." And he ran to Eli and said, "Here I am; you called me."

But Eli said, "I did not call; go back and lie down." So he went and lay down.

Again the LORD called, "Samuel!" And Samuel got up and went to Eli and said, "Here I am; you called me."

"My son," Eli said, "I did not call; go back and lie down."

Now Samuel did not yet know the LORD: The word of the LORD had not yet been revealed to him.

The LORD called Samuel a third time, and Samuel got up and went to Eli and said, "Here I am; you called me."

Then Eli realized that the LORD was calling the boy. So Eli told Samuel, "Go and lie down, and if he calls you, say, 'Speak, LORD, for your servant is listening.'" So Samuel went and lay down in his place.

The LORD came and stood there, calling as at the other times, "Samuel! Samuel!"

Then Samuel said, "Speak, for your servant is listening."

And the LORD said to Samuel: "See, I am about to do something in Israel that will make the ears of everyone who hears of it tingle. At that time I will carry out against Eli everything I spoke against his family—from beginning to end. For I told him that I would judge his family forever because of the sin he knew about; his sons made themselves contemptible, and he failed to restrain them. Therefore, I swore to the house of Eli, 'The guilt of Eli's house will never be atoned for by sacrifice or offering.'"

Samuel lay down until morning and then opened the doors of the house of the LORD. He was afraid to tell Eli the vision, but Eli called him and said, "Samuel, my son."

Samuel answered, "Here I am."

"What was it he said to you?" Eli asked. "Do not hide it from me. May God deal with you, be it ever so severely, if you hide from me anything he told you." So Samuel told him everything, hiding nothing from him. Then Eli said, "He is the LORD; let him do what is good in his eyes."[2]

The next night when Samuel lay near the ark of God, he felt different, as if he'd grown up in just one day. The Lord had visited him. The Lord had spoken important words and helped him deliver the message. Eli had listened and believed. Samuel curled up his legs and drifted toward sleep, no longer afraid and homesick.

Mama was right, thought Samuel. *I can trust God. He has things for me to do in His house.* He smiled his mother's radiant smile, thinking about what he'd tell her on the next visit. Then suddenly he slept, and in his dreams the temple echoed with his mother's girlish laugh.

A Heart in the Right Place

As Samuel pattered back and forth to Eli that night, his heart was in the right place, though his feet were not. The boy had not met God yet, nor could he discern the Lord's voice. So Samuel did what he knew to do—he obeyed the instructions of his old mentor—and God honored his sincerity. The Lord trusted the child with news that few adults could bear.

Learning to listen for God, we can feel as uncertain as Samuel, not yet able to discern His voice and consequently rustling around when we should be still. But as He was with Hannah's son, God is patient with our efforts, judging more by honest intentions than accurate interpretations. The Lord is kind and long-suffering, pleased with our desire to listen for Him, and understands that we'll make mistakes. As the Master Teacher, He allows His students the security of a lifelong learning curve. He praises our small steps.

Like Samuel, we can nurture the qualities that enable us to increase in discernment and faithfulness, prompting God to trust us with more of His messages. These qualities grow in believers who earnestly walk with God, gradually transforming our halting steps into a steady pace.

❧ *A childlike faith.* Jesus said, "I tell you the truth, anyone who will not receive the kingdom of God like a little child will never enter it" (Mark 10:15). Childlike faith anticipates God's written promises and trusts what He says to us personally. It doesn't complain, second-guess, or negotiate. Childlike faith believes.

As a young girl I experienced asthmatic attacks, and my mother remembers returning home from the store to discover me splayed on the front lawn, wheezing and needing oxygen. I recall having to give away the family dog and missing days at school. After months of worrying about me, my mother said, "I've had enough!" She'd read in the Bible about the Great Physician and decided He could heal me.

"In a way, I was too uninformed not to have faith in Scripture," explains my mother. "If the Bible said something, I believed it. I didn't know I could doubt what God told me in His Word." So every night before tucking me into bed, Mom and I asked Jesus to heal me. Not long after, the asthma cleared up.

The doctor said, "Sometimes kids grow out of these things."

My mom said, "Let's thank Jesus!"

Because of her childlike faith, I've never wheezed since.

❧ *A humble spirit.* The Lord said, "This is the one I esteem: he who is humble and contrite in spirit, and trembles at my word" (Isaiah 66:2). A humble spirit exalts the Lord rather than itself. Humility doesn't take pride in how frequently or accurately one hears from Him. A humble person realizes she is a vessel and reverently handles and communicates God's words.

When the angel announced to Mary that she'd bear the Messiah, she hurried to Elizabeth's home. But instead of talking about her "great future position" in the Kingdom as the Christ's mother, she glorified God with the poetic words:

> "My soul praises the Lord
>   and my spirit rejoices in God my Savior,
> for he has been mindful
>   of the humble state of his servant.
> From now on all generations will call me blessed,
>   for the Mighty One has done great things for me—
>   holy is his name.
> His mercy extends to those who fear him,
>   from generation to generation.
> He has performed mighty deeds with his arm;
>   he has scattered those who are proud in
>   their inmost thoughts.
> He has brought down rulers from their thrones
>   but has lifted up the humble.
> He has filled the hungry with good things
>   but has sent the rich away empty.
> He has helped his servant Israel,
>   remembering to be merciful
> to Abraham and his descendants forever,
>   even as he said to our fathers."
>
> Luke 1:46–55

When Mary heard from God, she focused on Him, understanding and acknowledging His power compared to her feeble humanity. She expressed gratitude for being a small part in His great, redemptive plan.

❦ *A submissive will.* The psalmist said, "Teach me to do your will, for you are my God; may your good Spirit lead me on level ground" (Psalm 143:10). A submissive will is quick to obey God's words, not with teeth-gritted obligation but with love for the Beloved. It focuses on the desire to please, not on the possible reward.

Not long after my friend Madalene's husband died, she sensed God's direction to sell their house and create a place for herself. She "house hunted" for a while, then decided that building a modest new home would be the best use of her money. Still grieving, she stored her belongings and lived with a daughter and her family, waiting out the start-and-stop delays of a construction project. More than a year later, Madalene moved into her new residence, finally able to "nest in" and start a new life.

"What a relief to have a place to call my own," she told me. "I love my kids, but I'm looking forward to being by myself." These were words uttered too soon. On the heels of her move, she heard God's request that she take in her troubled teenage granddaughter, acting as a guardian during the girl's last years of high school. Madalene had raised four lively children, and at age seventy she didn't relish becoming a taxi service and a disciplinarian again. But she loved her granddaughter, and she'd heard God's voice. To say no would be unthinkable.

For more than two years, raising a teenager was all-consuming and utterly challenging. The granddaughter had many character issues to work through, some quite serious. Madalene set aside her own pursuits and spent many hours training, counseling, disciplining, and praying for her granddaughter, and sometimes asking, "God, are You sure?" The answer was always yes.

A few months ago the granddaughter moved out to live on her own, with the grandmother's mission accomplished. Right now, Madalene doesn't know if the hard work will pay off in her granddaughter's character, and she continues to pray for and guide the young woman as needed. "It may take many years before there is deep and lasting change," says Madalene. "The point is, I did what God asked me to do."

When we hear God's voice, that is the point for us all.

An Ongoing Commitment

Of course, we don't acquire faith, humility, and submission all at once; they develop over time as we deepen our relationship with God. Still, we can imprint them on our minds, checking our attitudes against them as we listen for God's voice. We can also pray these words with the psalmist, as an ongoing commitment to listening with open ears and a pure heart:

Blessed is the man
who makes the LORD his trust,

who does not look to the proud,

to those who turn aside to false gods.

Many, O LORD my God,

are the wonders you have done.

The things you planned for us

no one can recount to you;

were I to speak and tell of them,

they would be too many to declare.

Sacrifice and offering you did not desire,

but my ears you have pierced;

burnt offerings and sin offerings you did not require.

Then I said, "Here I am, I have come—

it is written about me in the scroll.

I desire to do your will, O my God;

your law is within my heart."

I proclaim righteousness in the great assembly;

I do not seal my lips,

as you know, O LORD.

I do not hide your righteousness in my heart;

I speak of your faithfulness and salvation.

I do not conceal your love and your truth

from the great assembly.

Do not withhold your mercy from me, O LORD;

may your love and your truth always protect me.

Psalm 40:4–11, author's italics

The God of Many Chances

A young man was only thirty-two when he became a bank president. Surprised and uncertain about the new appointment, he visited his predecessor, the chairman of the board, and asked, "With your years of experience, could you give me some sound advice about how to succeed at this job?"

The old man looked at the new president and replied, "Right decisions!"

The young man wanted more explanation, so he asked again, "Could you be more specific? How can I make right decisions?"

The old man said, "Experience."

The new bank president, growing frustrated, tried again. "That's the point of my being here. I don't have experience, so how can I learn to do this job well?"

The chairman smiled and replied, "Wrong decisions!"[3]

The old bank chairman was wise and realistic, and we can apply his advice to our spiritual growth. We learn to hear God's voice through experience, and experience encompasses making mistakes. There is no way around this learn-as-you-go principle, and adopting its truth prompts us to relax rather than worry. Though we're to take seriously God's presence and relationship with us, though we're to diligently seek and carefully discern His voice, we're not communicating with a stern taskmaster. Again and again we need the reminder: God is our loving Father, applauding our tottering steps, supporting us when we fall, and helping us recover from mistakes.

However, if we're spiritually inattentive, God will jostle us. If we're compromising or disobedient in our walk, He will correct us. To ignore our waywardness would mean God is indifferent toward us, and this He can never be. Paul explained to the early church, "Our fathers disciplined us for a little while as they thought best; but God disciplines us for our good, that we may share in his holiness. No discipline seems pleasant at the time, but painful. Later on, however, it produces a harvest of righteousness and peace for those who have been trained by it" (Hebrews 12:10–11).

More than anything, God wants us to live in peaceful righteousness, able to enjoy and commune with Him. If we mis-hear or disobey His voice, galloping in the wrong direction and muddling up lives, there is restitution. When we repent, running back to Him for correction, we understand, yet again, the depth of His mercies. In the Father's arms, He offers us not what we deserve but what He desires.

❦ *Forgiveness.* "'No longer will a man teach his neighbor, or a man his brother, saying, "Know the LORD," because they will all know me, from the least of them to the greatest,' declares the LORD. 'For I will forgive their wickedness and will remember their sins no more'" (Jeremiah 31:34). Scripture is clear: If we confess and ask for forgiveness, God will forgive and forget our sins. From the misinformed mistake to the heinous defiance, His grace is excessive and sufficient to cleanse us when we falter. Even if God has been trying to tell us something for years and we've closed our ears, there is forgiveness when we repent.

We can remember, too, that not all missteps are deliberate disobediences. Especially when we're new to hearing God's voice (and even if we're seasoned at it), our actions can be well intentioned but misdirected. Or we may rush to do or say something without allowing God to guide or temper us. Or we may think we heard God when it wasn't Him at all. Every believer could tell stories about seeking God's voice and then messing up, and each one has been immediately offered His grace. The question is, Will we accept it? Even after God has forgiven us, we can be experts at punishing ourselves when we sin or merely goof. We need to forgive ourselves.

Scripture also tells us if we've offended and sinned against someone else, we're to ask that person for forgiveness too. Jesus said, "Therefore, if you are offering your gift at the altar and there remember that your brother has something against you, leave your gift there in front of the altar. First go and be reconciled to your brother; then come and offer your gift" (Matthew 5:23–24). Paul explained, "Bear with each other and forgive whatever grievances you may have against one another. Forgive as the Lord forgave you" (Colossians 3:13).

These instructions operate at both practical and spiritual levels. The practical: Seeking to hear from God and communicate the message to others, we all make mistakes, so we all need forgiveness. The spiritual: If we don't forgive, we will not be forgiven. Again, Jesus said, "Be merciful, just as your Father is merciful. Do not judge, and you will not be judged. Do not condemn, and you will not be condemned. Forgive, and you will be forgiven" (Luke 6:36–37).

In the spiritual realm, our choice to forgive is intertwined with the forgiveness granted to us. Consequently, if we've hurt someone with a misdirected, "Thus saith the Lord," or if we've tried to exercise control by saying, "God told me something about you," or our guidance pushes someone in the wrong direction, we are to ask that person for forgiveness. In turn, if this individual is a believer, God admonishes him or her to forgive us.

Charles Spurgeon, the renowned Victorian-era orator, advised his congregation: "One another! That means if you have to forgive today, it is very likely you will need to be forgiven tomorrow, for it is 'forgiving one another.' It is turn and turn about, a mutual operation, a cooperative service. In fact, it is a joint-stock business of mutual forgiveness, and members of Christian churches should take large shares in this concern. You forgive me, and I forgive you, and we forgive them, and they forgive us, and a circle of unlimited forbearance goes around the world.

"When we forgive, it is a poor and humble business compared with God's forgiving us, because we're only forgiving one another, that is, forgiving fellow-servants. Whereas, when God forgives us, it is the Judge of all the earth forgiving His rebel subjects, guilty of treason against His majesty. For God to forgive is something great. For us to forgive, though some think it great, should be regarded as a very small matter."[4]

🕯 *Restoration.* "If you repent, I will restore you that you may serve me; if you utter worthy, not worthless, words, you will be my spokesman" (Jeremiah 15:19). The Lord is not only the God of the second chance, He is the God of "umpteen" chances. In the Garden of Eden He launched a restoration business and has produced excellent work ever since.

When God forgives us, He plucks us from peril and accompanies us to a healing path. He restores some of us to our original calling, asking us to complete the obedience that we ignored. To others, He gives another chance through a different but similar avenue. Many times when God restores, He eventually blesses us beyond what we could imagine, if we continue following His way.

History records Teresa of Avila as a sixteenth-century Spanish nun devoted to prayer and able to miraculously hear from God. But Teresa didn't adopt the contemplative life without spiritual detours. After recovery from a prolonged mysterious illness she still diverted God's call to prayer. She wrote, "Who would have said I would fall so soon, after receiving so many favors from God, and after his Majesty had begun to grant me virtues which themselves aroused me to fear Him; after I had seen myself at death's door...after He had raised me up, in soul and body, so that all who saw me were amazed to see me alive? What it is, my Lord, to have to live a life so full of perils!"[5]

Teresa's convent was "more like a strictly run sorority house than a cloistered enclave,"[6] and she forsook solitude for socializing with visitors and trips home. We may not recognize her diversion as sin, but for twenty years Teresa made little spiritual progress because she shoved aside God's call. In her autobiography, Teresa recalls the frustration of living with a divided heart: "[It was] one of the most grievous kinds of life which I think can be imagined, for I had neither any joy in God nor any pleasure in the world."[7]

Then Teresa's father died, and a faithful friar became God's convicting voice to the frustrated nun. Francis, a Dominican friar, spoke to the grieving Teresa about her waywardness and handed her a copy of Augustine's *Confessions*. "Seeing herself in its pages, with abundant tears Teresa resolved to devote herself wholly to the Lord from that time on and, at the determined friar's insistence, resumed the practice of quiet prayer and never again abandoned it."[8]

❦ *Wisdom.* "For I will give you words and wisdom that none of your adversaries will be able to resist or contradict" (Luke 21:15). Recovering from mistakes and sin prompts us to learn "how not to do it next time," and hopefully the education instills wisdom and sharpens discernment.

A woman with a gift of discernment recalls this blundering incident that taught her wisdom: "During one particular prayer meeting, I was in rare form. A daughter of a friend of mine was visiting, and I discerned she had a drug problem. Without finding out anything about her situation, I pointed my finger at her and said with a loud voice full of drama, 'You have a demon of drugs!' Ouch! The girl completely freaked out. Her mother had worked with her for weeks to try to get her to attend church and I blew the whole thing."[9] Thankfully, today the woman is much wiser about the use of her gift.

Wisdom might also teach us that what seems like a mistake now, with hindsight, may be precisely what we were supposed to do. If we're disappointed from taking a risk or letting go of an opportunity, time may prove that we heard God's voice correctly. This kind of insight emerges from faithfulness, a daily plodding along when the view looks smoggy.

Missionary Ruthann Ridley describes the setbacks Donald Mac-Garvan faced after following God's voice:

Yale graduate Donald MacGarvan got up at dawn, ate a light breakfast, fixed his bicycle, and began his daily rounds. He pedaled several miles to the nearest village, wound his way through the pitiful market, and parked his bicycle in front of a dirty hut. Although they could offer him no refreshment, the young mother and father were glad he had come. They told him about their current landlord problems and discussed the famine. He stayed for a while, played with the baby, and tried to encourage them. Then he pedaled to another hut on the opposite side of town. He visited several villages that day and hurried home before dark to avoid robbers.

He had been a missionary in India for almost thirty years, and not much had happened, at least not from his point of view. His dream had been to see masses of people come to Christ all over the world. When he was a mission secretary, his superiors became annoyed with his extreme emphasis on evangelism. So they demoted him to the position of backwoods evangelist.

MacGarvan could have been discouraged. He could have become angry and bitter about the delay. Instead he persevered with the work he could do. Those years of patient endurance gave birth to the ideas that became his first book on church growth. Many more years of resistance to his call for evangelism in missions followed. Yet eventually his ideas took hold, and today few have influenced world evangelism as much as Donald MacGarvan.

God knew what kind of experience His man needed to accomplish his dream.[10]

🌶 *Renewal.* "Create in me a pure heart, O God, and renew a steadfast spirit within me" (Psalm 51:10). King David's prayer becomes meaningful when we're hurting from the embarrassment, disappoint-ment, or strained relationships caused by our sin and mistakes. If we keep our hearts tender, refusing to grow bitter or to blame God and others, our missteps can turn into spiritual renewal. We can dig deeper into God's love, grace, and guidance, carving new depth into our dependence on Him. We're never so willing to listen and obey as when we're in pain, and God uses these times to change and regenerate us. He refreshes the sorrowing soul.

So along with David, we can pray, "Let me hear joy and gladness; let the bones you have crushed rejoice. Hide your face from my sins and blot out all my iniquity. Create in me a pure heart, O God, and renew a steadfast spirit within me. Do not cast me from your presence or take your Holy Spirit from me. Restore to me the joy of your sal-vation and grant me a willing spirit, to sustain me. Then I will teach transgressors your ways, and sinners will turn back to you" (Psalm 51:8–13).

Actually, David's psalm forms a meaningful daily prayer for all who want to hear God's voice. It speaks of keeping our hearts pure, praising God's name, and drawing people to Him. In the end, whenever God speaks to us and however we respond, His ultimate goal is our soul's renewal. Then, in turn, we can become His mouthpiece in the world. And what better reason is there for hearing His gentle voice?

BIBLE
STUDIES

These in-depth, topical Bible studies will help you delve deeper into the scriptural principles presented in each corresponding chapter of *His Gentle Voice*. You may use them for individual study or with a small group, combined with the discussion questions beginning on page 229. You will need separate sheets of paper for your answers.

If you or your group have limited time available, break the studies (and discussion questions) into more manageable parts, completing only a third or half in each session. Or do only the questions that are most pertinent to you or the group.

Chapter One: The Hearing Heart

1. Read Hannah's story in 1 Samuel 1—2:11. Then consider these aspects about her quest to hear from God. Describe Hannah's attitudes toward her husband, his other wife, God, and Eli. Also describe their attitudes toward her.

2. Hannah hit barriers in her communication with God and waited a long time to receive a son. The Bible does not state the reason, but why would God delay His response? Name several possibilities.

3. Despite Hannah's bitterness and troubled emotions, God rewarded her. What does this reveal about His character?

4. When God answered Hannah's prayers, what was He possibly saying to her?

5. Consult these stories about God's communication with people in the Bible. What do they indicate about His desire to speak with humanity? State at least three assumptions.

- Genesis 3:8—9
- Leviticus 9:22—10:3
- Numbers 22:21—31
- Judges 6:36—40
- Daniel 5:1—9, 25—28
- Acts 9:1—8

6. The psalmists wrote about God's rule over the world and its people. Choose one of these passages (or all, if interest and time allow), and list the attributes of God found there. How could these attributes

affect our requests to hear from Him? State at least two ideas.

- Psalm 33:4–19
- Psalm 89:5–18
- Psalm 96

7. Now consider what God says about His dwelling places. With whom does God dwell? How could God's dwelling places affect His communication with us?

- Psalm 140:13, KJV
- Isaiah 57:15
- John 14:16–17
- Revelation 21:3

8. God says we are to search for Him. After reading these verses, what should characterize that search? What are the rewards of the search?

- Deuteronomy 4:29–31
- 1 Chronicles 16:10–11
- 1 Chronicles 28:9
- Isaiah 55:6
- Jeremiah 29:13–14

9. Even though God is present with us, why would He ask us to search for Him?

10. State, specifically, how searching for God could affect communication with Him.

11. If we're to hear from God, we need to believe He will speak to us. In these selected verses, what does the Bible say about belief?

- Mark 5:36

- Mark 11:23–24
- Acts 16:31
- Romans 19:9–10, 14

12. In these selections, what does the Bible say about faith?

- Matthew 9:27–30
- Matthew 17:20–21
- Romans 10:17
- Galatians 3:11
- Ephesians 2.8–9

13. Is there a difference between belief and faith? If so, what is it? If not, why?

14. Consider the previous verses (questions 11 and 12). How can belief/faith affect our communication with God?

15. John the Baptist emphasized the need for repentance before meeting Jesus. Read the story of Jesus' baptism and other verses about repentance. How is repentance related to our relationship with God and, consequently, to hearing from Him?

- Matthew 3:1–12
- Acts 17:24–30
- Romans 2:4–11
- 2 Corinthians 7:10

16. Sometimes we also have to wait before hearing from God. According to these verses, what are the rewards of waiting?

- Psalm 27:13–14
- Psalm 37:7, 34
- Psalm 40:1–2

- Proverbs 20:22
- Isaiah 40:31

17. In what ways could waiting affect a person's attitudes and character?

18. If God asks us to wait, how might it affect our opinion (negative or positive) of Him? How, specifically, can we overcome negative responses to waiting for God?

19. After reading these verses, answer the following questions. What is God's opinion of obedience? Why does He ask us to obey? How does obedience/disobedience affect our communication with God?

- Deuteronomy 11:26–28
- 1 Samuel 15:22
- Jeremiah 7:21–24
- Acts 5:29

20. What are human motivations for obedience? Would these motives affect hearing from God or discerning His voice? Why or why not?

❧

Chapter Two: The Divine Agenda

1. Why would God cast Himself as the Great Initiator?

2. In the following passages, briefly review some highlights of God's redemptive intent for humanity. What messages could these verses speak to us? List two or three.

- Isaiah 9:6–7

- Isaiah 53:1–6
- Luke 2:8–12
- Luke 4:16–19
- John 14:2–3
- 1 John 4:14–16

3. Read how the Lord initiated contact with these people from biblical times. What characteristics did these visits have in common? For example, consider the method of communication, the message He delivered, the person He communicated with, etc.

- Moses   Exodus 3:1–14; 4:1–17
- Jonah   Jonah 1:1–3:2
- Mary   Luke 2:26–38 (optional: verses 46–55)
- Zacchaeus   Luke 19:1–10

4. Review the Lord's message to each of these people. Describe how it was redemptive in nature. Whom was He desiring to save? From what? Were there any conditions?

5. Now compare the responses of the people with whom the Lord initiated conversations. How were their responses similar? How different? When they responded to the Lord, what was His reply?

6. What can these biblical people teach us about listening to God?

7. God delivers many types of redemptive messages to His children, some of which will be explored in the remainder of this session. But first, read Matthew 6:33. How could this instruction relate to our hearing messages from God?

8. The author gives examples of how God speaks the following

redemptive messages to us. For each of these messages, read the accompanying verses and explore the following questions. It may help to construct a chart to organize the answers:

Why would God condescend to speak this message to us?

Why is it important that we listen? What could happen if we don't?

What key words and phrases make this message especially poignant and/or comforting?

He expresses His love.

- Psalm 100:5; 117:2
- John 15:9–13
- Romans 8:38–39

He declares His presence.

- Deuteronomy 31:8
- Jeremiah 24:6
- Matthew 28:18–20

He comforts the soul.

- Psalm 34:17–20
- Isaiah 40:1–2
- Isaiah 66:12–13

He answers prayer.

- Matthew 6:6
- Matthew 7:7–11
- 1 Peter 3:12

He asks us to pray.

- Matthew 5:44

- Matthew 9:37–38
- James 5:16

He calls us to servanthood.

- Isaiah 41:9
- Mark 9:35
- 1 Peter 2:16

He gives us insight and wisdom.

- Proverbs 2:6–11
- Luke 2:52
- James 1:5

He guides our steps.

- Psalm 32:8
- Psalm 73:23–24
- John 16:13

He instills courage.

- Joshua 1:6–7; 23:6
- 1 Chronicles 28:20
- Hebrews 3:6

He prompts good works.

- Titus 3:8
- James 2:17–18
- 1 Peter 2:12

He reveals the future.

- Habakkuk 2:2–3
- John 16:25–33
- 1 Thessalonians 5:2–6

He warns about oppressors.

- Zechariah 9:8
- Matthew 7:15−16
- 1 Peter 5:8

He convicts the wayward.

- Isaiah 1:18−20
- Jeremiah 2:19
- John 16:7−11

He corrects our attitudes.

- Proverbs 3:11−12
- Matthew 12:33−37
- Hebrews 12:7−11

Based on this session, summarize the characteristics of God's redemptive messages.

Chapter Three: The Word Already Spoken

1. What does the Bible say about its author and origin? Is there a way we can prove these assertions? Explain.

- 2 Timothy 3:16a
- 2 Peter 1:16, 20−21

2. What does God say about the Scripture's ability to endure? Why is this quality crucial to its effectiveness?

- Matthew 5:18
- Matthew 24:35
- 1 Peter 1:25

3. According to these verses, what are some characteristics of God's Word? Why is each of these characteristics important to its existence?

- Psalm 12:6
- Psalm 18:30
- Psalm 93:5
- Psalm 111:7–8
- Proverbs 6:22–23
- John 17:17

4. What are some of the roles of God's Word in our lives? Are there other roles that could be added to this list? If so, look them up and write them out.

- Psalm 19:7–11
- Psalm 119:105
- Proverbs 6:20–22
- Isaiah 55:11
- 2 Timothy 3:16–17
- Hebrews 4:12–13

5. What should characterize our relationship to God's Word? Write a description.

- Deuteronomy 11:18–21
- Joshua 1:8
- Psalm 1:2
- Psalm 119:11
- Proverbs 7:1–3

6. Read Psalm 119. It will require some time, but it's rich in

insight and worth the effort. As you read through this meditation on God's Word, answer the questions below.

- In relationship to God's Word (the law), what does the psalmist promise to do or say we are to do? (Example: *Walk according to the law,* verse 1.)

- What does he ask the Lord to do? (Example: *Do good to your servant,* verse 17.)

- What benefits does the psalmist receive from God's Word? (Example: *Counsel,* verse 24.)

There will be numerous responses to each question, so it's helpful to create a chart with the titles "Our Actions," "Our Requests," "The Benefits," and then list the answers under the appropriate headings. Also, indicate the accompanying verse for each answer. Note the examples in parentheses after each question.

It may help to break the psalm into segments and study the verses over several days. It can be divided this way: 1) verses 1—40; 2) verses 41—80; 3) verses 81—120; 4) verses 121—152; 5) verses 153—176. In a small group, the verses can be divided among members, then shared with one another.

7. After studying the psalmist's meditation on the Word, do you think there is a relationship between our actions, our requests, and the Word's benefits to us? Explain.

8. Review the list "Our Requests." How can these requests turn into channels for hearing God's voice?

9. Look at the list "The Benefits." Which benefits could be synonymous with hearing God's voice? (Example: *God's statutes are*

our counselors, verse 24.)

10. Write a one-sentence summary of the Bible's relationship to hearing God's voice.

❧

Chapter Four: Listening to the Soul

1. Explore these passages and describe the various ways God's voice sounded when He spoke to biblical people.

- Deuteronomy 5:22—27
- 1 Kings 19:11—12
- Job 49:9
- Psalm 29:3—9
- Hebrews 12:25—27

2. From the previous passages, what is suggested about the sound of God's voice?

3. Consider again Elijah's unusual encounter with God's voice (1 Kings 19:11—14). After his triumph with the priests of Baal (1 Kings 18:16—46), why might the sound of God's voice be surprising in this passage?

4. We can hear God's still voice through the inner impressions of the soul. According to 1 Corinthians 2:9—10, 15—16, why is this possible?

5. According to the following verses, what biblical evidence suggests that God spoke to people through the Holy Spirit? Are there other examples in the Bible? If so, add them to the list.

- Luke 1:41—45
- Luke 1:57, 67

- Acts 11:12

6. The Scriptures below reveal the Holy Spirit's role in our lives. What are those roles? How do these relate to hearing God's voice?

- John 4:23—24
- John 14:27
- John 16:7—11
- Romans 8:2
- Romans 8:26—27
- 1 Corinthians 2:11—15
- Galatians 5:22—23
- Ephesians 4:3—4

7. What do these verses suggest about preparing our hearts to hear God's voice within?

- Psalm 85:8
- Psalm 95:7—8
- James 1:22—25

8. When we sense an inner impression of the soul, we aren't always sure it's God. The author suggests several ways we can determine whether it's Him. Read the biblical basis for her assertions, then answer these questions about each characteristic of God's voice.

- Why is this characteristic crucial to hearing from Him?
- What would be Satan's or man's counterpart to this characteristic?
- In what ways can you use this characteristic to discern whether God has spoken?

a. God speaks with clarity.

- John 10:1—5
- John 10:25—27

b. God's voice is specific.

- Isaiah 30:20—21
- Deuteronomy 8:1

c. God is not in a hurry.

- Nahum 1:3
- 2 Peter 3:8—9

d. God confirms His message.

- Romans 15:8
- Hebrews 2:2—4

e. God never contradicts His Word.

- Isaiah 40:8
- 2 Timothy 2:13

f. God's voice corrects instead of accuses.

- John 3:18
- Romans 8:1

g. God doesn't change His mind.

- Malachi 3:6
- Romans 11:29

9. Do all of these characteristics need to be present to hear God's voice? Why or why not?

10. Based on lessons one through four, when someone reads a Bible verse that seems like a *rhema* Scripture to her, how can she discern if this is true?

11. Why can we claim the promises of Scripture for our lives?

- 2 Corinthians 1:20
- Hebrews 6:11–12

12. What would be the benefits and pitfalls to claiming promises of Scripture for ourselves? Explain.

13. Compare how God communicated with these biblical people while they prayed. What were the similarities and differences in the methods and messages?

- Daniel   Daniel 6:6–11; 9:20–23
- Early Christians   Acts 4:23–31
- Peter   Acts 10:9–16

14. From the example of these people, how does a believer cultivate listening prayer (listening for God's voice in prayer)?

15. What is to be our attitude in listening prayer?

Chapter Five: The Meaning of Messengers

1. Messengers cross our paths in many ways. In these stories from David's life, where did the messengers originate?

- 1 Samuel 16:4–13
- 1 Samuel 20:12–23
- 1 Samuel 25:14–31

2. Describe the differences among the messengers in the previous stories. How was each one appropriate to the situation?

3. In these stories, what kind of messages did God's messengers bring?

4. What other kinds of messages could be added to this list? Give a biblical reference to support the answers.

5. God often uses people in our local community of believers to speak to us. What does the Bible say about developing spiritual community?

- Psalm 133:1
- Proverbs 27:17
- Hebrews 10:24–25

6. When believers gather together, either one-on-one or in groups, what are we to do?

- Psalm 118:1
- Psalm 119:16
- Romans 12:15
- Ephesians 5:19–20
- 1 Thessalonians 5:11
- 1 Thessalonians 5:17–18
- 1 Peter 4:9

7. Which of the previous activities would enable messengers to speak to us? Why?

8. Look up these verses and read the gifts of the Spirit. Which of these gifts could be employed to speak God's words to us? How?

- Romans 12:6–8
- 1 Corinthians 12:1–11, 27–30
- Ephesians 4:11–12
- 1 Peter 4:10–11

9. According to these passages, how are spiritual gifts to be used

in the Body of Christ? How does this function relate to being messengers to one another?

- Romans 12:3—6
- 1 Corinthians 12:12—26
- Ephesians 4:12—16

10. Choose two of these stories and compare and contrast the way
these people responded to God's messengers. What was God's
response to them?

- Sarah and Abraham   Genesis 18:1—19
- Lot and his wife   Genesis 19:1—29
- Jacob   Genesis 32:22—32
- King Asa   2 Chronicles 15:1—7, 16—19

11. God takes seriously our response to His messengers. Overall,
what are the results if we heed His voice? If we don't?

- Exodus 23:20—22
- Deuteronomy 11:26—28
- 1 Samuel 12:14—16

12. If we don't listen to God's messengers, but later repent, what is
our hope?

- Deuteronomy 30:8—10
- 2 Chronicles 7:14—15; 30:9
- Jeremiah 26:3—6

13. Obviously, not all messengers are from God. In these stories,
how were evil and deceptive forces involved in delivering messages?

- Genesis 3:1—7
- 1 Samuel 28:8—25

- Ezra 4

14. In what ways might Satan disguise himself as God's messenger today?

15. What are appropriate ways to respond to Satan's messengers?
    - Matthew 4:1–11
    - 1 Corinthians 10:13
    - James 4:7

16. Sometimes messengers can be well intentioned or motivated by what makes sense through human reasoning, but misguided in their words to us. Read these biblical incidences of misguided messengers.
    - For background, read Job 1:13–19. Then learn about the misguided messenger in Job 2:7–10.
    - Job 42:1–9
    - Matthew 16:21–23

   For each story, answer the following:
    - What might have motivated the(se) messenger(s)?
    - How did the recipient(s) respond?
    - What was the outcome of the message?

17. What guidelines has God given us to follow when we experience the pain of messy messengers?
    - Leviticus 19:18
    - Proverbs 24:28–29
    - Proverbs 25:21–22
    - Matthew 5:21–24
    - Matthew 5:38–42
    - Luke 17:3–4

18. According to Isaiah 43:10, in what way are we all God's messengers?

19. Read how these people responded when God called them to be messengers. What characterized their response? How did God respond? In what ways could their responses affect their ability to be messengers?

- 1 Samuel 3:1—10
- Isaiah 6
- Jeremiah 1

20. Based on this session and the verses below, summarize the responsibilities of being a messenger.

- Exodus 6:29—7:2
- Ephesians 4:15, 25

Chapter Six: When Heaven Comes Calling

1. What are the reasons God uses the extraordinary to get people's attention?

- Psalm 66:1—4
- John 2:11, 23
- John 14:11
- Romans 15:18—19
- Hebrews 2:1—4

2. Psalmists often wrote about the glory of nature. In these passages, what does nature tell us about God?

- Psalm 19:1—4

- Psalm 24:1—2
- Psalm 97:1—7

3. In the Bible, what are some ways God bent the laws of nature to speak to people?

- Exodus 14:19—28
- Exodus 17:3—7
- Joshua 10:12—14
- 2 Kings 20:1—11
- John 11:38—44

4. How might God miraculously use nature to speak to us today?

5. How might He use the ordinary aspects of nature to speak to us? Describe a specific example.

6. What assurances does God give us that He will guide us? After reading the verses below, write out a one-sentence promise from God about His intent to guide us.

- Psalm 25:8—10
- Isaiah 58:11

7. Explore the ways God guided these people through circumstances. What were the circumstances that changed their lives? At the time, could they tell God arranged these circumstances? Why or why not?

- Ruth   Ruth 1; 4:1—10
- King Josiah   2 Kings 22:1, 8—20

8. On the other hand, in these stories the circumstances were orchestrated by craftily motivated people. What characterized these circumstances?

- Jacob   Genesis 29:15—30
- Joseph   Genesis 37:12—28

9. In the previous stories, how did God exemplify the truth of Romans 8:28? What does the outcome reveal about God's relationship to all circumstances?

- Jacob   Genesis 35:23—26 (The twelve tribes of Israel)
- Joseph   Genesis 45:1—10

10. Compare the circumstances from God with those that were manipulated by humans. What cues can you glean about discerning whether circumstances are from Him?

11. What could be the advantages and pitfalls of depending on circumstances as a way to hear God's voice?

12. Read about Abraham's servant Eliezer who chose Rebekah for Isaac's wife in Genesis 24:12—26. He asked God for a circumstantial sign to guide him. Is this a valid way to search for God's voice today? Why or why not?

13. Throughout the Bible, God spoke to people through angels. After reviewing these stories, write a description that answers, "Why would God use angels instead of human messengers?"

- Gideon   Judges 6:1—16
- Zechariah   Luke 1:8—19
- Jesus   Luke 22:39—46

14. In other extraordinary incidences, God used dreams and visions to speak. Read the following stories and speculate about these questions:

- Why would God use this means to communicate the particular message?
- How could the individual determine that the dream/vision was from God?
- In what way was this dream/vision life changing?
- Jacob   Genesis 28:10−15
- Ezekiel   Ezekiel 1:1; 2−3:9
- Amos   Amos 7:1−9
- Joseph   Matthew 1:18−22
- Paul   Acts 18:9
- John   Revelation 1:1−3, 9−19

15. How can we determine whether a dream or vision is from God?

16. God also spoke audibly to people of biblical times. Read about two of these occurrences, and give an opinion: Why do people not hear God's audible voice today?

- Abraham   Genesis 12:1−4
- John the Baptist and crowd   Matthew 3:13−17

17. In the Bible God performed many miracles, but He also used people to present the miraculous. In the following incidences, what did God accomplish with miracles performed through His people? What was the message that God may have been speaking to the recipients?

- David   1 Samuel 17:41−50
- Elisha   2 Kings 4:1−7
- Apostles   Acts 5:12−16
- Paul   Acts 19:11−12

18. Why would God choose to use people to perform His miracles?

19. Read in Exodus 7:14–22 and 2 Thessalonians 2:7–11 about counterfeit miracles. Specifically, how could a Christian test whether a miracle is from God or a counterfeit?

20. Do you think God still performs the miraculous today? Justify your answer.

21. When God speaks through the extraordinary, what should be our attitude and action?

🌿

Chapter Seven: Breaking Down the Barriers

1. According to Ephesians 6:12, what kind of battle is the Christian engaged in?

2. Read 2 Corinthians 4:3–4. How has this battle affected people's ability to communicate with God?

3. Satan rules the evil spiritual world and is known by many names. What do these verses reveal about his character?[1]

- Genesis 3:1
- Genesis 3:13
- Psalm 8:2
- Isaiah 54:16
- Matthew 4:3; 1 Thessalonians 3:5
- Matthew 6:13; John 17:15
- Matthew 12:24
- John 8:44
- 2 Corinthians 4:4
- 2 Corinthians 11:14

- Ephesians 2:2
- Revelation 12:7—9
- Revelation 12:10

4. Knowing Satan's character, state three specific examples of how he tries thwarting God's communication with us.

5. When facing spiritual warfare, what can we remember?
- Isaiah 41:13
- Hebrews 2:14—15
- 1 John 4:1—4

6. What weapons do we carry against the onslaughts of Satan and his intent to destroy our communication with God?
- 2 Chronicles 20:21—22
- Matthew 16:19
- Matthew 18:19—20
- Ephesians 6:10—18
- Philippians 4:4—7
- Revelation 12:10—11

7. Look again at the armor of God detailed in Ephesians 6:10—18. For each part of the armor, name two specific and practical ways to "put on" this piece of spiritual clothing.
- belt of truth
- breastplate of righteousness
- feet fitted with gospel of peace
- shield of faith
- helmet of salvation
- sword of the Spirit

8. How would each piece of the spiritual armor affect our communication with God, especially our ability to hear His voice?

9. In addition to this armor, how do we battle and defeat the enemy?

- James 4:7–10
- 1 Peter 5:8

10. There are also "preventive measures" we can take to quell the enemy, so we are not victims of attack. What are they?

- Deuteronomy 30:14–16
- Romans 8:26–27
- 1 Corinthians 3:16–17
- 2 Corinthians 9:26–27
- 2 Corinthians 10:5
- Ephesians 4:22–23
- Ephesians 4:26—27
- Ephesians 5:17–18
- 1 Thessalonians 5:17
- 1 Thessalonians 5:22
- 2 Timothy 2:3–4
- Hebrews 10:23

11. Ezekiel told the Israelites they would learn to discern between the "holy and profane," and the "unclean and the clean" (Ezekiel 44:23, KJV). According to John 14:26, how do we practice this discernment today?

12. When we're under severe spiritual attack, what else can we do? See Isaiah 58:6–9.

13. Read excerpts from the stories of Deborah (Judges 4) and

Esther (Esther 3—4, 7), biblical women engaged in physical and spiritual battle. Then ponder the following:

• In the text, what indicates each woman recognized her circumstances as a spiritual battle?

• What steps did each woman take to engage in spiritual warfare?

• How did each woman listen to God's voice?

• What character qualities did Deborah and Esther exude during these circumstances? Why were these qualities important?

14. The Bible says we're not to sin and give the devil a foothold in our lives (Ephesians 4:26—27). To keep from sin, how do we manage our fleshly natures and stay open to God's voice?

• Romans 6:19

• Romans 8:12—14

• Romans 13:3—4

• Galatians 2:20—21

15. If we sin, what happens to our communication with God? What will restore that communication?

• Psalm 66:18

• 1 John 1:9

16. If we are caught in habitual sin, what further spiritual warfare may be necessary to loosen Satan's grip and clear the passageways to God's voice?

• Exodus 20:5

• Ephesians 4:25—27

17. Read David's prayer of repentance from sin in Psalm 51. Write

out the key phrases David uttered that would restore his communication with God.

18. Romans 6:15—18 tells how obedience relates to our struggle against Satan and sin. What is the connection?

19. In all of our battles, what can we remember from Romans 8:37?

20. When we've done everything we know to unlock God's voice—and we still don't hear anything—what do we need to understand? Read Psalm 37 and write out all of the statements that answer this question.

≶

Chapter Eight: Praise for Small Steps

1. Review the story of young Samuel and the first time he heard God's voice in 1 Samuel 3:1—10. Though Samuel missed responding to God's voice three times, why would the Lord still wait for the boy? Consider both God's motive and Samuel's attitude.

2. Finish Samuel's story in verses 11—21. God didn't let any of Samuel's words "fall to the ground" (verse 19). To receive this honor, what type of person would Samuel have been?

3. The author suggests that three qualities are important to hearing God's voice. They are faith, humility, and submission. How are these qualities interrelated? How are they distinct from one another?

4. Jesus talked about childlike faith in the following passages. What are the distinctives of this type of faith?

- Mark 10:13—16
- Luke 9:46—48

5. Why would this type of faith be crucial to hearing God's voice?

6. The Bible also speaks about humility in our relationship to God. After reading these verses, summarize what He says about pride and humility.

- Proverbs 6:16–19
- Proverbs 16:18–19
- Proverbs 29:23
- Micah 6:8
- 1 Peter 5:5–6

7. If we're walking humbly before God, what words would describe our relationship and communication with Him? What words would describe us if we're wrapped in pride?

8. When we hear God's voice, He asks for our submission to His requests. Based on James 4:6–10, why is our submission (surrender) important?

9. How might we tell if we're approaching God with an attitude of submission? Name at least three telltale signs.

10. Sometimes when we fail to submit to God's way, He disciplines us. Paul wrote to the Hebrews about the reason for and the results of God's discipline of us. Read Hebrews 12:5–11 and then write a definition of God's discipline. What is it? What is its purpose?

11. Paul explained that God's discipline creates the "harvest of righteousness and peace" (verse 11). Write out definitions for peace and righteousness. How do each of these qualities affect our communication with God?

12. During times of discipline, what can we depend on from God?

- Psalm 37:24
- Psalm 94:12—15

13. If we've missed hearing or following God's voice, in what ways can we embrace forgiveness?
   - Psalm 86:5
   - Matthew 6:14—15
   - Ephesians 4:32

14. According to Psalm 103:11—12, when we are forgiven by God for our sins and mistakes, what does He do? List the descriptions of God's forgiveness in verses 3—18.

15. Name three ways we can follow God's example and forgive ourselves.

16. When we make mistakes and learn from them, we gain wisdom. According to Proverbs 3, what are the benefits of wisdom?

17. Leaf through the Bible study pages of this book. Gleaning from all eight sessions, what wisdom do we need to apply to listening for God's voice?

18. Again, based on all eight sessions, answer these questions with a personal opinion. For each answer, give an example from Scripture.
   - Why is it crucial to listen for God's voice?
   - What is the most important thing to remember about listening for God's voice?
   - What is the most important thing to remember when God speaks to us?

DISCUSSION
QUESTIONS

With a few friends or your small group, use these life-related questions to discuss and apply the principles in this book. Or if you prefer, combine them with the previous Bible study sessions.

If you or your group has limited time available, break the discussion questions (and the Bible studies) into more manageable parts, completing only a third or half in each session. Or do only the questions that are most pertinent to you or the group.

≈

Chapter One: The Hearing Heart

1. Can you identify with Hannah's desperation to hear from God? If so, describe a time when you felt this way. What did you do? What was the outcome?

2. The author says, "A vital relationship with God holds these two perspectives in balance: understanding that God is not bound by our opinions about how and when He should speak, but knowing He desires to talk with us." Understanding these two principles, what would you say to God if you were asking Him to speak to you?

3. Specifically, how can you tell whether your desire to hear from God is based on self-motivated goals or God's agenda? Name a few ways you can discern your motives.

4. How do you feel about God's requirement that you search for Him? Is there a difference between searching for God and seeking His voice? If so, explain.

5. Regarding hearing from God, do you ever struggle with unbelief? Why or why not? How can you increase your faith in God and His ways of communication?

6. What role has repentance played in your ability to hear from God?

7. Why would God ask you to wait to hear from Him?

8. Have you ever heard from God but didn't want to obey what He said? Describe what that felt like and how you managed your reluctance.

9. For you, what is the most important element of cultivating a hearing heart?

10. After reading this chapter, what questions still linger about being the kind of person God will speak to?

✎

Chapter Two: The Divine Agenda

1. Think of a time when God initiated communication with you. Explain how this differed from your initiating communication with Him.

2. In the past, how has God spoken to you about redemption?

3. What redemptive message do you need from Him today?

4. This chapter mentions many types of messages that God speaks to people. Do you think all Christians, at one time or another, would eventually receive all of these kinds of messages (love, His presence, comfort, answered prayer, a request to intercede, a call to servanthood, insight and wisdom, guidance, courage, good works, revealing the future, warning about oppressors, conviction, correction, perseverance)? Why or why not?

5. What types of messages would you add to the list in question four?

6. Which type of message from God means the most to you? Why? Describe a time when you received such a message from God. Or, if you haven't heard this kind of message, why would you like to?

7. Some Christians always seem to be hearing from God. Others rarely do. What are the possible reasons for this difference?

8. What is your initial response when someone says, "God told me..."? Why do you respond this way?

9. Do you ever dread or fear hearing from God? What is the source of this feeling?

10. What can you do to be reassured that God speaks to you with love and with your best interest in mind?

*

Chapter Three: The Word Already Spoken

1. How did God's Word play a part in your initially giving your life to Him?

2. Compare how the Bible spoke to you as a new Christian and how it speaks to you now. What is similar? What is different?

3. In what practical ways do these assertions affect your life?

- The Bible is God's Word.
- The Scriptures always endure.
- The Bible speaks the truth.
- God's Word doesn't change.
- The Scriptures are reliable.

4. Do you ever have trouble embracing any of these previous facts about the Bible? If so, which one(s)? Why?

5. Which of these five facts about the Bible means the most to you? Why?

6. If you could only choose one type of verse—manna or arsenal—to speak to you, which would you select? Why?

7. Which types of verses most frequently speak to you—manna

or arsenal? Explain and give examples.

8. The author says, "In many instances we don't need to implore God because it'd be asking Him to state the obvious. We only need to recall or look up what the Bible says." Do you agree? Why or why not?

9. What is your favorite way to dig for insight from the Bible?

10. Name a topic on which the Bible is silent but you'd like to determine God's mind about it. Do you think it's possible to know what God thinks about it? Explain.

Chapter Four: Listening to the Soul

1. When God speaks to you personally, what does His voice usually sound like?

2. When you think God is speaking directly to your soul (an inner impression), how do you know He is the One speaking?

3. Describe the most poignant time when God spoke personally to you. What did you learn from it?

4. Describe a time you thought God spoke directly to you and it probably wasn't Him. What did you learn from this episode?

5. What kinds of abuses can result from people who claim they hear from God but don't? How can you guard against these abuses?

6. For you, what is the best way to confirm whether God has spoken to you?

7. How do you know God has given a *rhema* verse to you?

8. Share a time when you received a *rhema* verse. What was the outcome?

9. Have you ever practiced listening prayer? Describe how this process operates for you.

10. Do you have concerns about listening for God through inner impressions? Do these misgivings need to be resolved or used as cautionary guidelines?

☙

Chapter Five: The Meaning of Messengers

1. What is the allure of hearing from God through a messenger?

2. What are your reservations about hearing from God through a messenger?

3. How can you determine whether a messenger is reliable?

4. Who in your community of friends and family could be a reliable messenger for you?

5. Is it possible to ask someone to be a messenger to you? Or should messages always be unsolicited?

6. Which spiritual gifts do you think are most often employed by messengers (administration, apostle, discerning of spirits, exhortation, evangelist, faith, giving, healing, helps, interpretation of tongues, knowledge, leadership, mercy, miracles, shepherding [pastor], prophecy, service, teaching, tongues, wisdom)? Why?

7. How can we guard against looking for a message from a certain spiritual gift rather than looking to God?

8. Why are words from messengers sometimes painful?

9. Can messy messengers be avoided? Explain.

10. Do you want to be a messenger? Why or why not?

&

Chapter Six: When Heaven Comes Calling

1. Why are we both drawn to and skeptical about the extraordinary ways God might use to communicate with us?

2. What are the benefits and pitfalls of hearing from God through uncommon means?

3. Of the extraordinary means of communication mentioned in this chapter, which do you most readily believe and receive (nature, circumstances, angels, dreams, visions, miracles)? Why?

4. Which means of communication are you most skeptical about? Why?

5. Why would God use the extraordinary to speak to people?

6. Do you think God uses extraordinary methods frequently or infrequently? Explain.

7. If you've heard from God through any of the methods presented in this chapter, describe it to the group. What did you learn from this experience?

8. Do you believe that God still performs miracles? Explain your answer.

9. Has anyone you've known said she experienced the miraculous? Tell the story and explain your response to it.

10. What is the most important thing to remember when God uses the extraordinary to communicate with us?

❧

Chapter Seven: Breaking Down the Barriers

1. Have you ever hit a wall of silence while trying to hear from God? What did it feel like?

2. On a scale of one to ten, how aware are you of spiritual warfare in your life? "1" = "Not at all," and "10" = "Always aware." Give examples.

3. Satan likes to attack us where we are most vulnerable (examples: fear, worry, anger, etc.). Have you experienced being hit where you're vulnerable when trying to hear from God? What happened?

4. The author suggests several indicators of spiritual warfare (negativity about a specific issue; general sense of despair; intensity of emotion; strife; addiction; isolation; accusations; inability to relate to God; confusion; emotional paralysis). How else can you discern if you're being attacked in the spiritual realm?

5. From the book, read the description of the armor of God on page 16. What, specifically, could you do each day to put on this armor?

6. If you're wondering if sin might be a barrier between you and God but aren't sure if it is, how could you discern this?

7. How could generational sins (sins inherited from the fathers and mothers) affect your ability to hear from God?

8. Which barriers to hearing God's voice do you struggle with the most: busyness; completing what you've already been told to do; emotional injuries; physical factors? Discuss specific ways to overcome your barriers.

9. If you haven't heard from God, what is your natural response? If this response is negative or self-blaming, how can you dissolve it?

10. Do you think there is a way to know if God is saying, to wait? Explain.

&

Chapter Eight: Praise for Small Steps

1. What are your uncertainties about seeking to hear from God? Explain.

2. Which of these ways resemble your relationship with God as you seek to hear from Him? Why do you feel this way?

- A loving partnership.
- Trying to get an inattentive parent's attention.
- Feeling like "the problem" is always me.
- Talking to a blank wall.

3. Describe what you'd like your communication with God to feel like.

4. What do you think is the main key to hearing from God?

5. What does childlike faith mean to you? Describe a situation (not from the book) that exemplifies childlike faith.

6. Is a humble heart a quality we can seek, or does God give it to us? Explain, with examples.

7. Why is it sometimes difficult to have a submissive will toward God's plan?

8. Is there a way you can grow secure in God's forgiveness and His

willingness to offer you a second chance when you fail? If so, what would it be?

9. Which do you need most from God right now: forgiveness, restoration, or renewal? If you feel comfortable doing so, explain why.

10. In what ways has God used you as His mouthpiece in the world? How would you like for Him to use you as His mouthpiece?

Notes

❧

Introduction

1. Frank S. Mead, ed., *The Encyclopedia of Religious Quotations* (Old Tappan, N. J.: Fleming H. Revell Company, 1965), 213.

Chapter One: The Hearing Heart

1. 1 Samuel 1:7, 9–18.
2. 1 Samuel 1:19–20, 24–28; 2:11.
3. Henry T. Blackaby and Claude V. King, *Experiencing God* (Nashville: LifeWay Press, 1990), 18.
4. D. W. Lambert, *Oswald Chambers: An Unbribed Soul* (Fort Washington, Pa.: Christian Literature Crusade, 1983), 7.

Chapter Two: The Divine Agenda

1. Blackaby and King, *Experiencing God*, 28.
2. Corrie ten Boom, *Not good if Detached* (Fort Washington, PA: Christian Literature Crusade, 1957), 94–95. Used by permission of Baker Book House Company.
3. Quoted in Robert Veninga, *A Gift of Hope* (Boston: Little, Brown and Company), 214.
4. Dutch Sheets, *Intercessory Prayer* (Ventura, Calif.: Regal Books, 1996), 84.
5. Cheri Fuller, *When Mothers Pray* (Sisters, Ore.: Multnomah Publishers, 1997), 124.
6. Bob Benson, *He Speaks Softly* (Dallas: Word Books, 1985), 21–2.

Chapter Three: The Word Already Spoken

1. John Bunyan, *The Pilgrim's Progress* (1678, reprint, New York: Holt, Rinehart and Winston, 1961), 10–4. Slightly edited for readability.
2. C. S. Lewis, *Mere Christianity* (New York: Macmillan Publishing Co., Inc., 1977), 174.
3. Ibid., 173–4.
4. Information from the Internet website, http://www.bible.com/answers/afacts.html.

5. Quoted in Kay Arthur, *Lord, I Want to Know You* (Sisters, Ore.: Multnomah Books, 1992), 63.

6. Information from The Dead Sea Scrolls Foundation at the Internet website, http://www.hum.huji.ac.il/staff/fdss.htm.

7. Information from the Internet website, htttp://www.webzone.net/block/William%20Tyndale.html.

8. Information from the Internet website, http://www.bible.com/answers/afacts.html.

9. Information from the Internet website, http://www.bible.ca/b-archeology.htm.

10. Information from the Internet website, http://www.bible.ca/b-divine-human-origin.htm.

11. Quoted in Calvin Miller, *A Hunger for Meaning* (Downers Grove, Ill.: InterVarsity Press, 1984), 64.

12. John Sherrill, *My Friend, the Bible* (Lincoln, Va.: Chosen Books, 1978), 55–6.

13. Information from the Internet website, http://www.bible.ca/b-pyramid-seed.htm.

14. Author unknown. Quoted in M. Scott Peck, M.D., *In Search of Stones* (New York: Hyperion, 1995), 219.

15. Evelyn Christenson, *Lord, Change Me!* (Wheaton, Ill.: Victor Books, 1977), 69–70.

Chapter Four: Listening to the Soul

1. Corrie ten Boom, *Not Good If Detached* (Fort Washington, Pa.: Christian Literature Crusade, 1957), 65–7. Used by permission of Baker Book House Company.

2. Charles Colson, *Transforming Society* (Colorado Springs: NavPress, 1988), 15–6.

3. A. W. Tozer, *I Talk Back to the Devil!* (Camp Hill, Pa.: Christian Publications, 1990), 6.

4. Amy Carmichael, *Candles in the Dark* (Fort Washington, Pa.: Christian Literature Crusade, 1982), 7.

5. John Wesley, quoted in Debra Evans, *Six Qualities of Women of Character* (Grand Rapids: Zondervan Publishing House, 1996).

Chapter Five: The Meaning of Messengers

1. Don Richardson, *Eternity in Their Hearts* (Ventura, Calif.: Regal Books,

1981), 73–5, 92–4. Used by permission.

2. See Romans 12:4–8; Ephesians 4:11–14; 1 Corinthians 12–14; 1 Peter 4:10–11.

3. Explanations in parentheses taken from C. Peter Wagner, *Your Spiritual Gifts Can Help Your Church Grow* (Ventura, Calif.: Regal Books, 1979), 59–60.

4. Sophocles, *The Dramas of Sophocles,* trans. Sir George Young (1888), 16.

5. Charles Dickens, *A Tale of Two Cities* (Norwalk, Conn.: The Eaton Press, 1981), 22.

Chapter Six: When Heaven Comes Calling

1. Rebecca Ruter Springer, *Intra Muros* (Forest Grove, Ore.: Book Searchers, n. d.), 46–53.

2. Calvin Miller, *A Hunger for Meaning* (Downers Grove, Ill.: InterVarsity Press, 1984), 77–8.

3. Cicero, *De Divinatione,* Book II.

4. Lois Trigg Chaplin, *A Garden's Blessings* (Minneapolis: Augsburg, 1993), no page available.

5. Gerard Manley Hopkins, "God's Grandeur," *England in Literature* (Dallas: Scott Foresman and Company, 1973), 407.

6. Frederick William Robertson, quoted in *The Encyclopedia of Religious Quotations,* ed. Mead, 307.

7. Paul Meier, M.D. and Robert Wise, Ph.D, *Windows of the Soul* (Nashville: Thomas Nelson Publishers, 1995), 159.

8. Ibid., 12–3.

9. Judith Couchman, *Designing a Woman's Life* (Sisters, Ore.: Questar Publishers, 1995), 74–5.

10. Amy Carmichael, *Things As They Are* (out of print), quoted in Corrie ten Boom, *Plenty for Everyone* (Fort Washington, Pa.: Christian Literature Crusade, 1967), 122–4.

Chapter Seven: Breaking Down the Barriers

1. C. S. Lewis, *The Screwtape Letters* (New York: Macmillan, 1961), 3.

2. Quin Sherrer and Ruthanne Garlock, *A Woman's Guide to Spiritual Warfare* (Ann Arbor, Mich.: Servant Publications, 1991), 31.

3. Ibid.

4. Dwight L. Moody, *Only Trust Him,* comp. Judith Couchman (Ann Arbor, Mich.: Servant Publications, 1998), no page available.

5. Ramona Cramer Tucker, ed., *The Busy Woman's Guide to a Balanced Life* (Wheaton, Ill.: Tyndale House Publishers, Inc., 1997), 153.

6. Elisabeth Elliot, *Discipline: The Glad Surrender* (Old Tappan, N.J.: Fleming H. Revell Company, 1982), 40.

7. Cindy Jacobs, *The Voice of God* (Ventura, Calif.: Regal Books, 1995), 66.

8. Ibid., 69.

Chapter Eight: Praise for Small Steps

1. 1 Samuel 3:1–3.

2. 1 Samuel 3:4–18.

3. Author unknown, told by Medard Laz, *Love Adds a Little Chocolate* (Ann Arbor, Mich.: Charis Books/Servant Publications, 1997), 129.

4. Charles Spurgeon, "Forgiveness Made Easy," *For Me to Live Is Christ*, comp. Judith Couchman (Ann Arbor, Mich.: Servant Publications, 1998), no page available.

5. Teresa of Avila, *The Life of Teresa of Jesus: The Autobiography of Teresa of Avila* (New York: Image/Doubleday, 1991), 69.

6. Debra Evans, *Six Qualities of Women of Character* (Grand Rapids: Zondervan Publishing House, 1996), 142.

7. Teresa of Avila, *The Life of Teresa of Jesus*, 109.

8. Evans, *Six Qualities of Women of Character*, 143.

9. Jacobs, *The Voice of God*, 111.

10. Ruthann Ridley, "The Great Wait," *Discipleship Journal*, issue 36, 1986, 37–38.

Bible Study, Chapter Seven

1. Scripture list from Sherrer and Garlock, *A Woman's Guide to Spiritual Warfare*, 33–4.

About the Author

Judith Couchman owns Judith & Company and works as an author, editor, and speaker. She is the author or compiler of twenty-two books and has published many magazine articles and curricula pieces.

Judith was the creator and founding editor-in-chief of *Clarity,* a magazine for Christian and spiritually seeking women, and has served in editorial and management positions in publishing and organizational communications.

Judith has received national recognition for her work in education, public relations, and publishing and holds an M.A. in journalism and a B.S. in education. She is an avid flower gardener and an occasional art history student at a local university.

She lives in Colorado.

To learn more about Judith's books and speaking,
visit her web site on the Internet at
http://www.judithcouchman.com